25

DUMFRIES
&
GALLOWAY

25 WALKS

DUMFRIES & GALLOWAY

TOM WHITTY

SERIES EDITOR: ROGER SMITH

MERCAT

www.mercatpress.com

First published 1995 by HMSO
This revised edition published in 2007 by Mercat Press
10 Coates Crescent, Edinburgh EH3 7AL
www.mercatpress.com

ISBN13: 978-1-84183-118-1

Maps reproduced by permission of Ordnance Survey
© Crown Copyright 2007
Ordnance Survey Licence number 100031557

Printed and bound in Great Britain by Bell & Bain Ltd.

CONTENTS

PRACTICAL INFORMATION

The length of each walk is given in kilometres and miles, but within the text, measurements are metric for simplicity. The walks are described in detail and are supported by the appropriate section of Ordnance Survey maps with the route marked out, which you should study before you start the walk. There should be little chance of going astray, but if you want a back-up, take an Ordnance Survey 1:50000 Landranger or 1:25000 Explorer map with you. The maps are at various scales, but in every case the sides of the blue squares represent one kilometre.

Every care has been taken to make the walk descriptions and maps as accurate as possible, but the author and publishers can accept no responsibility for errors, however caused. The countryside is always changing and there will inevitably be alterations to some aspects of these walks as time passes. The publishers and author would be happy to receive comments and suggested alterations for future editions of the book.

Access in Scotland

The Land Reform Act came into full effect in Scotland in February 2005. The Act gives the public a general right of access to all open countryside in Scotland, with the provisio that this access must be exercised responsibly. There are exceptions to the general right such as in the vicinity of houses or other buildings, on industrial sites, airports and railway lines, and military areas. Access rights can be temporarily suspended for activities such as shooting or timber felling.

The rights and responsibilities of the public and of land managers are explained in the Scottish Outdoor Access Code which can be found at: www.outdooraccess-scotland.com. Simplified versions of the Code are available in leaflet form (Know the Code Before You Go) at Tourist Information Centres or from Scottish Natural Heritage (www.snh.gov.uk). The principal points emphasised in the Code are as follows:

- Take personal responsibility for your own actions, and act safely
- Respect people's privacy and peace of mind
- Help land managers and others to work safely and effectively
- Care for your environment and take your litter home
- Keep your dog under proper control
- Take extra care if you are organising an event or running a business.

Most of the walks in this book are along well-established routes and there should be no difficulties encountered.

Dogs and Livestock

Dogs must always be kept under close control in the countryside, and we recommend that dogs are not taken on walks in livestock areas, and particularly not during lambing and calving times (notably in the spring between March and May).

A number of the walks in this book pass through livestock areas where sheep or cattle may be encountered. This should not cause any particular problem, but again, please go quietly in these areas and take every care not to disturb livestock, on which the farmer's livelihood depends.

Gates

The general advice with farm gates is to leave them as you find them. If a gate is closed, shut it carefully and securely behind you. Please be scrupulous about this: carelessly leaving a gate open may lead to stock getting into the wrong field and cause the farmer a great deal of difficulty. It also gives walkers a bad name. If a gate is open, this is for a reason, and it should be left open.

Litter

We do ask walkers to be absolutely scrupulous about not leaving litter, and indeed to help reduce this pernicious problem by picking up litter that others have left. Your help in this is much appreciated.

General Information

Information on the Dumfries and Galloway area can be obtained via the VisitScotland website at www.visitscotland.com, where you will find clear links to the area, these in turn leading to more detailed information. You can also try the VS information line on 0845 22 55 121.

The main tourist information centre for the area is at 64 Whitesands, Dumfries DG1 2RS, and enquiries may be made by post or by email to info@dgtb.visitscotland.com This TIC is open all year. There are seven other TICs in the area, as follows:

- Markethill car park, Castle Douglas DG7 1AE
  castledouglas@dgtb.visitscotland.com
- Car park, Gatehouse of Fleet DG7 5EA
  gatehouseoffleet@dgtb.visitscotland.com
- Unit 10, Gretna Gateway Outlet Village, Gretna DG16 5GG
  gretnagreen@dgtb.visitscotland.com
- Harbour Square, Kirkcudbright DG6 4HY
  kirkcudbright@dgtb.visitscotland.com
- Churchgate, Moffat DG10 9EG
  moffat@dgtb.visitscotland.com
- Dashwood Square, Newton Stewart DG8 6EQ
  newtonstewart@dgtb.visitscotland.com
- Burns House, 28 Harbour Street, Stranraer DG9 7RA
  stranraer@dgtb.visitscotland.com

Some of these TICs are only open seasonally (Easter to October).

Countryside and access information is also available through the website of Dumfries and Galloway Council at www.dumgal.gov.uk. The Southern Upland Way long distance route crosses the whole region and its website is at www.dumgal.gov.uk/southernuplandway. The official guide to the Way, published by Mercat Press (www.mercatpress.com), contains details of a large number of shorter walks which use parts of the Way.

There are many forest walks in the area, for details contact the Forestry Commission, South Scotland Conservancy, 55-57 Moffat Road, Dumfries DG1 1NP, 01387 272440, southscotland.cons@forestry.gsi.gov.uk.

Information and contact details specific to particular walks are given in the information panel for that walk.

Public transport

While we would wish to encourage walkers to use buses and trains whenever possible, it has to be said that relatively few of the walks in this book are easily accessible by public transport. Details of bus services in the area can be obtained through tourist information centres, from the bus station in Dumfries, or via the National Traveline on 0870 608 2 608 or www.travelinescotland.com, which contains full timetable information. Some bus services do not run or may have reduced frequency on Sundays: check your information before setting out.

There are rail stations at Dumfries, Lockerbie, Stranraer, Sanquhar and Annan. For details of services contact the national rail enquiry line on 08457 48 49 50, go to www.firstscotrail.com or enquire at stations.

INTRODUCTION

I jumped at the chance to write this book. What a great opportunity, I thought, to promote the Southern Upland Way. After 13 years as ranger for the western section of this under-used national trail, perhaps I could be forgiven for clutching at straws.

So, 25 walks in Dumfries and Galloway? Yes, please. I'll do it! Within minutes of accepting the offer I had my 25 all worked out, starting on the Southern Upland Way in the far west and finishing, still on the Southern Upland Way, to the east of Moffat. High profile promotion means more people. More people mean greater economic benefits which in turn lead to more finance, more staff. In short, I thought *25 Walks* could be the key to unlocking years of chicken-and-egg deadlock.

It was not to be. My wife and common sense—not a partnership to be trifled with—intervened. 'Don't you think there's more to walking in Dumfries and Galloway than the Southern Upland Way?'

My children were no more sympathetic: 'Get a life, Dad. You're a deviant.' My brainwave transpired to be no more than self-centred exploitation.

I gave in. Better to opt for a variety of routes: some short, some long, some south, some north, some woodland, some moor, some coastal, some... Well, the list is endless. The south-west corner of Scotland has an almost infinite variety of places to walk. How is a body supposed to choose?

This problem was compounded by recent events. First I had Tom Prentice's original edition of *25 Walks* to work from—all excellent routes, covering Dumfries and Galloway without hint of linear distribution. Add to this the hard graft of Council Access Teams across the region, establishing paths where no path went before. Finally, the recent arrival of Land Management Contracts offers land managers financial incentives for public access. By now, 25 walks could hardly scratch the surface.

The premise that footpaths can be graded according to difficulty gave one key: everyone who picks up the book should find a

few paths they really like the look of, and some a bit more testing. Dumfries and Galloway probably has four categories. There's: 'can be tricky'—call this category A; 'a bit of a scramble'—B; 'not for faint-hearts'—C; and finally 'only for goats'. Call that last one category D.

The great thing about the Southern Upland Way, I can't help pointing out, is that it encompasses all four categories equally well. But by this time I had decided for reasons of purity to miss out the long-distance route altogether, concentrating my efforts on describing walks of varying length and difficulty. Self-denial is a horrible thing.

The coast is excellent and infinitely variable in its own right. You could easily dedicate 25 walks to the shores of the Solway. Then there are the ranges of hills: the Lowthers, the Merrick etc. It would be unforgivable to miss them out. What about inland lochs? The bottom line is, almost anywhere you go in Dumfries and Galloway, you'll find a great walk. And best of all, it's quiet. If you wish, you can walk all day and meet no one.

Dumfries and Galloway is like a secret. It's a place of rugged, breathtaking hills, perhaps not quite as rugged and breathtaking as those to the south of the Solway; of beautiful stretches of coast, maybe not quite as picture-postcard as parts of Argyll; of little towns not quite managing to turn themselves into quaint tourist honeypots. It is the antithesis of humdrum, of high tech, of hype. And so, to date, its prodigious landscape assets are accentuated by its quietness and qualities of untrammelled wildness. Snow can lie undisturbed on an upland path for a week. Your feet, apart from the prints of a mountain hare, are the first to mark it. Here, unlike so many other rural parts of the United Kingdom, you can experience the luxury of being absolutely alone.

While I remember, I must add a note of thanks to those who have helped me with this book. Tom Prentice for his excellent work on the first edition. All farmers and landowners who listened to my proposals without showing me the door. My wife, Marion, for constructive criticism—it was like having a shave with one of those multi-bladed safety razors; not really life-threatening, but a lot more painful than the packaging led me to believe, and great for removing the fluff! Members of the Dumfriesshire and Galloway Historical and Antiquarian Society for specialist information. And, of course, my daughter Rachel, for lending me her digital camera.

As the list of walks took shape, I became vaguely aware of a disconcerting thing happening. The Southern Upland Way began to creep back onto the agenda. In early drafts it appeared in lower case letters, as if to avoid detection. It's a subliminal thing. Once or twice I even omitted mentioning the fact that as you follow the directions in the text, turning off the public road or the forest track, you are actually joining the coast-to-coast national trail. I think I've put it right now, but in the original draft you could have identified it by my sudden use of superlatives: 'turn right down a most inviting little path which runs between copses of native, wildlife-abundant semi-natural oak woodland'.

I've had a great time putting these walks together. I hope you get equal pleasure following them.

Roads and Paths

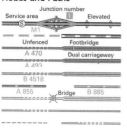

Motorway (dual carriageway)	
Motorway under construction	
Primary Route	
Main road	
Secondary road	
Narrow road with passing places	
Road generally more than 4m wide	
Road generally less than 4m wide	
Path / Other road, drive or track	
Gradient: 20% (1 in 5) and steeper, 14% (1 in 7) to 20% (1 in 5)	

Railways

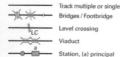

Track multiple or single
Bridges / Footbridge
Level crossing
Viaduct
Station, (a) principal

Water Features

Rock Features and Heights

Contours are at 10 metres vertical interval
Heights are to the nearest metre above mean sea level
·144
Heights shown close to a triangulation pillar refer to the ground at the base of the pillar and not necessarily to the summit.

Land Features

Quarry
Spoil heap, refuse tip
Coniferous wood
Non-coniferous wood
Mixed wood
Orchard
Forestry Commission access land
National Trust for Scotland

ruin
Buildings
Public building (selected)
Bus or coach station
Place of worship { with tower / with spire / without }
Chimney or tower
Triangulation pillar
Mast
Wind pump

Tourist Information

⚠	Camp site
🚐	Caravan site
✿	Garden
⚑	Golf course or links
i i	Information centre
⚘	Nature reserve
P P+R PaR	Parking, Park and ride
✗	Picnic site
	Selected places of tourist interest
✆ ✆	Telephone
☼	Viewpoint
V	Visitor centre
!	Walks / Trails
▲	Youth hostel

Antiquities

+	Site of monument
· o	Stone monument
⚔	Battlefield (with date)
☆ ····	Visible earthwork
VILLA	Roman
Castle	Non-Roman

Abbreviations

P	Post office
PC	Public convenience
PH	Public house
TH	Town Hall
CG	Coastguard
CH	Clubhouse
MP	Milepost
MS	Milestone

Walk Symbols

Start of walk
Walk route
Direction of walk
Southern Upland Way

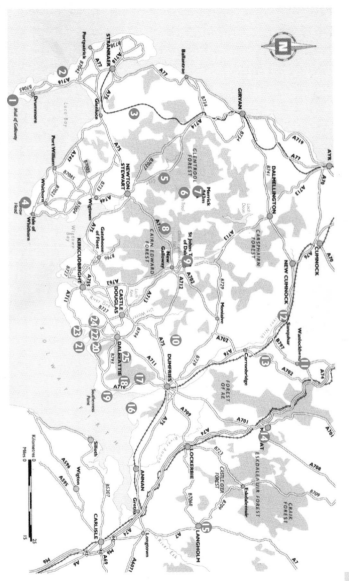

MULL

Lagvag

6

85

Start/Finish

Cairn

15

D

16

6

Earthwork

56

Kennedy's Cairn

14

Gallie Craig

East Tarbet

21

30

40

54

37

Cairngaan

Mull of Galloway Fm

Cave

Standing Stone

Homestead

West Tarbet

Fort

Forts

13

1 km

Crown Copyright 100031557

Distance	4 km (2.5 miles) circular.
Start and Finish	Mull of Galloway lighthouse car park. From Stranraer take the A716 south, or from the A75 at Glenluce take the A715 until it joins the A716, continuing to Drummore. Then take the B7041, signposted for the Mull.
Terrain	Cliff-top paths and grazed fields. Boots or strong shoes recommended.
Map	OS Explorer 309, Stranraer & The Rhins.
Refreshments	Mull of Galloway Coffee House. Drummore has shops and pubs.
Opening Hours	Lighthouse: Apr–Sept, Sat & Sun, 10.00–15.30. Entry fee. Mull Visitor Centre: Apr–Oct, daily 10.00–16.00. Free.

Scotland's most southerly tip is the Mull of Galloway. 'Mull' comes from Maol, the Gaelic word for bare. At a first glance the visitor would probably agree; apart from the white lighthouse there appears to be nothing much there. The Mull is just a barren, windswept headland of grazed turf. After half an hour's drive down The Rhins from Stranraer you may start wondering why you bothered. But persevere, it's worth it.

Much of the interest of the Mull is centred on the lighthouse, built in 1828 by Robert Stevenson at a cost of £9,000. For incoming ships it marks the southernmost tip of the Solway's north shore while also providing a bearing for northbound shipping heading for the Clyde or Loch Ryan. Moreover it warns of the dangerous seas around the Mull. Not only is there a fierce tidal race, but the location of the light enables shipping to avoid the Scare Rocks—disappointingly pronounced 'Scar'—lying unlit in the middle of Luce Bay. Robert Stevenson built 23 lighthouses. He was Chief Engineer to the Northern Lighthouse Board for 47 years. The author, Robert Louis Stevenson, was his grandson.

Around the lighthouse are various points of interest: a well house, a redundant walled garden, the lighthouse keeper's cottages and the fog-horn, which might be supposed to be the Mull's chief attraction, going by the number of signs pointing to it. The views include the coast of Northern

Ireland, the Isle of Man and, along the Galloway coast, Burrow Head. The Merrick and other Galloway hills create a towering backdrop.

The RSPB visitor centre is housed in a traditional cottage. It provides information about the nature reserve. You can learn which birds to watch out for and how old the rocks are. There is a very nice picture of the last of the lighthouse keepers and family, before two million candlepower was entrusted to automation.

Having completed the short circular walk via the visitor centre and lighthouse, you can turn left off the road just below the Coffee House and walk on the sea side of the fence along the cliff top for a few hundred metres. It's easy going. If you've no head for heights keep within the fence and follow it round, but for the best look at nesting or perching birds and the closest eyeballing of some very good rock formations you need to be on the cliff edge.

The stock fences are a recent addition to the Mull. Too many cows missed their step and took nose-dives. The fences don't add much to the place but the farmer has been very generous with kissing gates. Where one appears, turn right towards a stone monument to a Mr Kennedy. Some-one, perhaps Mr Kennedy himself, had the bright idea of building stone steps into this edifice, so that you can climb it and survey the surrounding countryside.

Carry on downhill as far as the first of two earthworks, formed by gouging out trenches and using the dug material to pile up walls. Once completed these were probably topped by wooden palisades and would have effectively cut off the Mull from the rest of the Rhins, safeguarding whatever animals and people were within. If this is an Iron Age fort it is one of the biggest in Britain and achieved with minimal work, as the cliffs on all other sides give natural protection.

Follow the first earthwork to the right until you hit the road, where another right turn takes you back in the direction of the car park. The Coffee House offers superb views and a spectacular 30-metre fall from the balcony into a churning Irish Sea. I admit once refusing to enter because it involved spending money. This wasn't through any half-baked ideas that every walking experience has to be free, but simply because I hadn't got any. I missed out, not only on a very good cup of tea but also on experiencing one of the most courageous farm diversification

South side of the Mull

schemes the area has to offer. The very modern look to this café, its excellent position on the cliff top and its turf-roofed blending with its surroundings must put it at the cutting edge of tea-room evolution. Some people walk right past it and never realise it's there.

The Mull is a great place for a stroll. Close-cropped turf, grand cliffs, interesting wildlife and awe-inspiring geology. There's also enough salt spray coming up from below to give spectacle lenses a fine white coating so you think the light level is going down and the day spoiling until you remember to give them a wipe. This is a short walk and totally undemanding, but none the worse for that.

Mull of Galloway Lighthouse

ARDWELL

Distance	Short walk: 3km (2 miles); longer walk: 7km (4.5 miles). Both circular.
Start and Finish	Ardwell Bay car park. From Stranraer take A716 south, or take the A715 from near Glenluce, joining the A716 near Sandhead. Continue through Sandhead, then turn right on a minor road signposted Kirkmadrine Stones, Clachanmore and High Ardwell. At the end of the minor road, continue along a rough track to the car park at the end of the beach.
Terrain	Sand, shingle, grazed farmland, farm track and minor public road. Boots or strong shoes recommended.
Map	OS Explorer 309, Stranraer & The Rhins.
Refreshments	None nearby.
Other Interest	The Kirkmadrine Stones can be seen behind glass at Kirkmadrine Church. These are some of the oldest Christian monuments in Scotland.

The chief reason for visiting Ardwell is the broch. Up the north-west coast of Scotland brochs are two-a-penny, but in Dumfries and Galloway they're rare. To my mind, Ardwell is the best local example. It doesn't tower 15 metres high and have the distinctive, almost industrial appearance of the Broch of Mousa on Shetland. It doesn't tower at all; it's just a pile of stones. But that's not the point. The very fact that a broch stood here is enough to fire the imagination. Besides which, some of the lower stonework is in its original condition: dry-built block precision-laid upon dry-built block, 2,000 years after the craftsmen set them in place.

From Ardwell Bay, follow the path across a stile heading roughly south with the sea on your right. You come to the broch almost immediately. Look for a natural defensive position on a spit of rock, jutting out into the sea. Reaching the monument from the landward side involves crossing a narrow rock causeway. The site is ideal in other ways: try to land a boat there and you'd turn it to matchwood.

Almost always by the sea, brochs are always round and always twin-skinned. Usually they are built where the local stone forms straight-edged blocks, aiding their dry-stone construction. So similar are the

nuances of building technique that the production of the 500 or so recorded brochs is thought to have been a family affair. A patent defensible homestead, perfected and proved against sea-borne troublemakers, would have appealed to most. The tribe of broch builders thus had several centuries' guaranteed employment. South of Carlisle, however, their services were not required—the Romans had everything pretty well sewn up.

In general shape, a broch defies easy description: a sort of tapering cylinder with inward curving sides, a bit like a power station cooling tower. In spite of the walls containing passages and stone staircases, the profile was admirably stable. Internal space may have been floored, as in later tower houses, or there may have been tiered systems of strut-supported wooden galleries. Livestock would likely occupy the ground floor in times of trouble.

Debate continues over what happened at the top. To my mind, anyone ingenious enough to produce such a building could hardly stop short of putting on a roof of some sort, though this would have had dire consequences for ventilation and lighting.

Coast, north of Ardwell Bay

Ardwell Broch has a landward and a seaward entrance. This is very rare and not ideal for defensive purposes. Perhaps Ardwell's second doorway was added at a later date. Archaeological digs inside brochs show them to have been inhabited and vacated several times over the course of centuries so it's not unreasonable to suppose improvements were made by later dwellers, possibly after the buildings' defensive purpose had lapsed.

Return to the cliff top and follow a signposted path inside the fence. Keep Slunk Cottage on your right, heading for South Ardwell Farm where you need to turn left along the track to the

Clachanmore Phone Box

tarred road. Having seen the broch, you could now return to your car. However, if the day is young, exercise is needed and you'd like to see a bit more of Ardwell, turn right at the ruinous shed and walk along the quiet public road to Clachanmore. It's about 1.5km.

When you get to Clachanmore there's an old schoolhouse with double crow-stepped gable ends and the dates of active service, 1875-1962. And a phone box. Not any ordinary phone box, but one of the rare red-painted classics. At a time when you can hardly be considered human if not carrying a mobile phone with picture-taking capability and internet access, these quality phone boxes are as anachronistic as brochs and as endangered as red squirrels. For conservation purposes, it could be considered a matter of principle never to walk past one without making a call. Why? Because, apart from the usual vandals, you may be the only one to lift the receiver this financial year. Cost-cutting executives in high places will mutter in dismay: 'Damn and blast! Some idiot's using the Clachanmore Box!' Removal will be unjustifiable.

Retrace your steps a hundred metres, turning right at Low Ardwell Farm back towards the sea. This lane comes out at Saltpans Cottage, on the beach. Turn left now to return to your car. The walk ends along a very nice stretch of shore with wide views along the coast and beady-eyed oystercatchers for company. You can either walk along the shingle, scrambling over rocks, or you can try to keep above the beach where there are remnants of a path, but it's pretty hard going. If there's a spring tide and a westerly gale blowing you probably won't have a choice.

Front door, Ardwell Broch

THE CAVES OF KILHERN

Distance	9km (5.5 miles) circular; or 11km (6.5 miles) if you visit the kist.
Start and Finish	New Luce Village Hall. Turn off the A75 at the west end of Glenluce, taking the minor road north past Glenluce Abbey.
Terrain	Minor road, grazed farmland and hill tracks. Boots recommended.
Map	OS Explorer 310, Glenluce and Kirkcowan.
Refreshments	Kenmuir Arms Hotel, New Luce.
Other Interest	Glenluce Abbey : open all year although times/days vary with season. Entry fee.

So that you won't be seen frustratedly roaming the moors, I should say that 'caves' is something of a misnomer. The area around New Luce is not limestone country. The underlying rock is solid stuff: graywacke. It doesn't lend itself to the formation of subterranean caverns.

From New Luce, walk 1.5km along the road towards Glenluce, joining the Southern Upland Way at Cruise Farm. If you wish you can precede the main walk by turning off to the right, following the Way westwards down the fields to the river, crossing the wobbly suspension bridge and the railway and finding a Waymerks kist in the woods.

Waymerks is a project unique to the Southern Upland Way. Thirteen artists were commissioned to make containers for specially minted tokens, called merks (the original merk was a Medieval Scottish coin). For Waymerks, a different coin was minted for each kist. Find the kist and you can take a merk. The kists are often hard to find. To save despondency, small metal 'Ultreia' tags are fixed to waymarkers either side of the kist. Ultreia means something like 'keep searching'.

The main walk is a circuit. Take the rough track running uphill, just opposite Cruise Farm. Once on the moor, follow an old drove road. This straight, raised highway would have been used for stock movement to and from remote pastures. Its construction over deep peat is an enigma. How was it floated? Sometimes such roads were supported on bundles of branches or reeds, which did not decompose due to the anaerobic conditions of peat bogs. Another technique was to use 'dirty wool'—the daggings from

Kilhern

the back end of sheep which have no natural appeal to knitters. Whatever was used in this case, it's proved a remarkably durable base.

The ruinous remains of Kilhern come into view as you top a rise. The farm was last lived in during the early 1960s by a world-renowned sheepdog breeder. Even with rapid improvements in transport, Kilhern would have been a remote, difficult place to farm. There may have been difficulties with the water supply, hence the pump shed below the house and the tall brick tank-tower. Peat saturates during the winter, but in a dry summer the water table can drop away quickly.

At the back of the steading you can find a levelled circle approximately 8 metres across, edged by a low wall. It's a horse-mill. One horsepower turned a central capstan, a crown and pinion wheel—often the back axle of an old car. A drive shaft conveyed this power through a hole in the barn wall to a threshing machine or some other labour-saving device. Kilhern is a snapshot of technological advance.

Follow the track northwards, sloughing off a millennium with every hundred metres' progress, arriving at the Caves of Kilhern and 3000BC simultaneously. You could cut a corner and go via the archaeological dig, surrounded by chestnut paling fence. To stay dry, remain on the track until you approach a gateway, then turn right alongside the wall among bracken. The Caves are 250 metres along, and consist of a low mound lying parallel to the dyke.

This is an example of a chambered cairn, tomb of Neolithic chieftains. The general idea was to bury deceased chiefs in mounds of stones. This was more laborious than interment, but nothing like as elaborate as the burial rites of contemporary Egyptians. In the mound, a burial kist would be formed by positioning larger stones in a box shape. The chief and some possessions would be ceremoniously interred. More stones covered the kist to deter thieves. The next chief to die would prompt an elongation of the mound, his kist being positioned just along from the first.

Further along the Way, hut circles can be found just to the left of the path, opposite a larch plantation. They can be hard to locate if the bracken is tall. Start at the waymarker and walk 50 metres perpendicular to the dyke. Early farmers lived here under turf roofs.

Fauldinchie Farmstead, 200 metres downhill, is a later relic: a perfectly preserved post-medieval settlement consisting of two buildings and a corn-drying kiln around which are extensive traces of rig and furrow cultivation and an enclosed field system. This farmstead was abandoned about the same time Henry VIII was on to wife number six. Intact remains as good as these are rare, existing only in areas of very low agricultural intensity.

Last relic: a burnt mound lies off the track to the right, 50 metres before you reach the road, beside a stunted hawthorn and a small watercourse. The smooth, crescent-shaped mound measures maybe 7 metres across and consists of a grass-covered pile of fire-blackened rocks. Cooking in Neolithic times, without fireproof vessels, required the direct heating of stones in fire. These were put into dammed water at the burn's edge, which boiled and could be used for cooking meat or washing clothes, or both. The used stones were tossed behind, forming distinctive heaps. This example represents hundreds of years of Neolithic hot dinners.

Turn left when you get to the road, following it down into New Luce.

The Caves of Kilhern, with Artfield Fell wind farm in the background

WALK 3

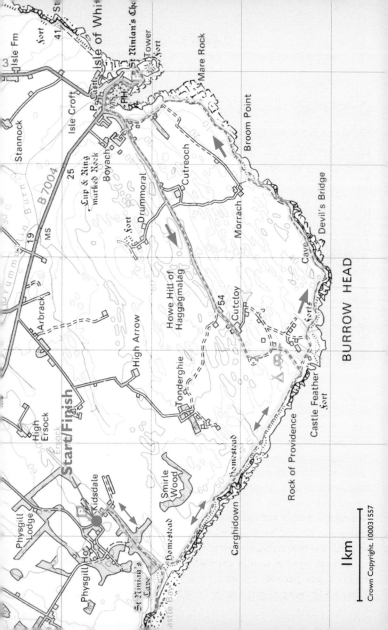

Crown Copyright. I00031557

1 km

BURROW HEAD

Start/Finish

Physgill Lodge
Physgill Ho
High Ersock
Arbrack
Stannock
Isle Fm
Fort
41
3
Isle of White
St Ninian's Cho
Tower
Fort
Mare Rock
Broom Point
Isle Croft
PH
Port Castle Bay
Boyach
Cutreoch
Morrach
Devil's Bridge
Cave
Drummoral
Fort
Cup & Ring
marked Rock
B7004
25
19
MS
Kidsdale
Smirle Wood
St Ninian's
Cave
Castle Bay
Carghidown
Homestead
Rock of Providence
Castle Feather
Fort
Forts
Cutcloy
54
Howe Hill of
Haggagmalag
High Arrow
Tonderghie
Homestead

ST NINIAN'S CAVE AND CHAPEL

Distance	St Ninian's Cave and return: 3km (2 miles). St Ninian's Cave to St Ninian's Chapel: 10km (6 miles) linear. St Ninian's Cave and Chapel return: 20km (12 miles). If you're making the return trip you might consider taking the road back from the Isle of Whithorn to Burrow Head Holiday Camp. It only takes half the time.
Start and Finish	Kidsdale car park. Take the A714 south from Newton Stewart to Wigtown, then the A746 through Whithorn. Turn left onto B7004 and after 1.5km/1 mile turn right on a minor road signposted Kidsdale. If you want to leave return transport at the Isle of Whithorn, it's straight on along the B7004.
Terrain	Tracks, shingle beach, cliff-top path and grazed farmland. Some cliff-top path sections are the seaward side of a stock fence. Boots or strong shoes recommended.
Map	OS Explorer 311, Wigtown, Whithorn & The Machars.
Refreshments	Reasonable choice in Whithorn. Pubs on the Isle. Toilets: In Whithorn.
Toilets	In Whithorn
Opening Hours	Whithorn Visitor Centre, 'The Whithorn Story': displays and tours. Open Apr-Oct daily 10.30–17.00. Admission charge.

In the centuries after Christ there were quantities of rival saints humming around, vying with one another to spread Christianity across Europe. From some accounts, these iconic bringers of peace and goodwill were highly competitive. For example, two saints, Moluag and Columba, raced each other across Loch Linnhe to claim an island domain. Moluag, having chosen the slower boat and perceiving he was falling behind, resorted to cutting off his finger and throwing it on the beach, so as to have got there first. Seeing the finger hit the shingle, Columba accepted defeat with bad grace, turned his boat and went off in a rage. He had to make do with a different island—Iona.

This glimpse of saintly animosity puts Bishop Nynia's achievements in perspective. Because it was from Ad Candida Casa, Saint Ninian's Shining White House at Whithorn, that Christianity is known to have spread throughout Scotland, Ninian was first and most important of all Scotland's saints. After his death in 432 AD his name and various abodes continued to dominate the locality. Several hundred years later, when Norse invaders arrived, they accepted the established brand, calling this bottom tip of the machars Hwiterne or Hvitsborg, both meaning 'White House'. The current placename's derivation is apparent.

In common with other saints, Ninian had an isolated place of retreat for prayer and reflection. When life's niggling problems got too much for him, he'd disappear from the humdrum of work to go and ask God's advice. Some saints had stone chairs in out-of-the-way places, which would be all very well unless it was raining. St Ninian's refuge was more practical: a cave. From about the 8th century onwards, this cave and the chapel on the Isle of Whithorn became important places of Christian pilgrimage. Stones and crosses dating from the period, discovered in the cave by 19th-century archaeologists, are now in the Whithorn Priory Museum.

The way down to St Ninian's Cave is signposted. However, the signage can get overgrown in the summer and isn't all that obvious, so to save you standing in the road looking mystified, turn left out of the car park, pass Kidsdale Farm, then take a path down a burn running between trees, just after a house on the right. This burn starts small and grows in size. You expect some significant outpouring into the sea, but when you arrive at the beach the water mysteriously disappears into a 2 metre mound of shingle and

a forest of poisonous hemlock water dropwort.

At the beach turn right again and walk 300 metres to the cave, where there is an interpretation plaque. That's about it. It's not luxurious, as caves go. There are no stone seats, no chimney, nor

St Ninian's Cave

Ponds near Burrow Head

even obvious ledges upon which to put a candle. You can't help wondering, in the few seconds it takes you to look around, what pilgrims down the centuries made of it. Some came long distances on foot, others travelled perilously by sea. Kings came, and paupers. While one might expect a holy man's bolthole to be humble, it is a bit of an anticlimax.

Rugged coasts often have interesting names. Round the corner from Port Castle Bay is Bloody Neuk. All sorts of munitions are washed up on Galloway's coast, due to the fact that after the Second World War the military decided sea burial was a good way of getting rid of stockpiled explosives. They dumped them in Beaufort's Dyke, a deep channel off The Rhins, but it wasn't deep enough, and rusty cylindrical lumps of iron found on the beach are better left alone. As for Bloody Neuk; it sounds like the horrified exclamation of someone finding more than the usual phosphorous flares. Actually, it's just a deep indentation in the cliff, immediately behind St Ninian's Cave.

If it was a short walk you wanted, return the way you came, but if you want to trace St Ninian's steps between workplace and refuge you need to return along the beach to the south-east end and take the cliff-top path, established here by a Solway Heritage task force in the 1990s. Among the dramatic rock formations along this stretch are two Ducker's Rocks, perhaps alternative venues for testing the credentials of witches, one Devil's Arch and the Rock of Providence.

Follow the path until you cross a dyke, slightly inland of the cliff edge. You'd think you were miles from the nearest habitation, but suddenly the tell-tale oblongs of mobile homes appear. This is Burrow Head holiday village. In the war it used to be an artillery camp, hence the scattering of concrete buildings. For gunnery practice, a drogue, or target, would be towed behind a plane or boat, the object being to knock out the drogue without hitting the tug. What St Ninian would have made of it all, if he had wandered along the coast a few centuries out of context, is anyone's guess. The same might be said for the holiday camp, with its indoor and outdoor swimming facilities and luxury homes on wheels.

Continue along the increasingly spectacular coast path from Burrow Head round to the Isle. Locals have walked here for years, but only recently have there been measures to establish a proper footpath. A succession of galvanised kissing gates mark the route. This development says a lot for the ambitious path-creation programme drawn up by Council Access Officers, and for the farmers who have agreed to formalise footpaths.

Round the harbour, you'll come upon St Ninian's Chapel among small fenced fields. It's humble, like his cave. Dating from around 1300, it probably replaced an earlier wooden structure. If the existing building is anything like the original, it strengthens the impression that Ninian wasn't a man keen on excess.

You have now completed the foot journey St Ninian made, coming back from his place of refuge to the workplace. But Ninian never had the problem of having left his transport at the other end—he probably didn't walk both ways on the same day. Unless, of course, things at the workplace were so bad when he arrived, he just turned on his heel and left them to it.

St Ninian's refuge to St Ninian's Chapel is quite a step in itself, let alone if you walk all the way back again. With a bit of forethought you can save yourself the return journey. Large parties should take two cars, allowing one to be left at either end.

Isle of Whithorn

Then most of you can make merry in the Queen's Arms while martyred drivers set off to retrieve transport. Single car and bike does just as well. Leave a bike at the Isle of Whithorn, then flip a coin for who takes it back to Kidsdale, while the rest ditto the Queen's Arms.

WALK 4

19

WATER OF MINNOCH

Distance	9km (5.5 miles) circular.
Start and Finish	Lay-by next to the village hall at Bargrennan, 13km/8 miles north of Newton Stewart on the A714 Girvan road.
Terrain	Woodland path, machine paths, minor roads. Boots or strong shoes recommended.
Map	OS Outdoor Leisure 32, Galloway Forest Park or OS Explorer 319.
Refreshments	House o' Hill Hotel, Bargrennan or Stroan Bridge Forestry Commission Visitor Centre (turn right at Glentrool Village, signposted Bruce's Stone and Loch Trool).
Opening Hours	Apr–Oct: 10.30–16.00.
Information	Newton Stewart Tourist Information Centre is open Mar–Oct: 10.00–16.00.

Starting at the hamlet of Bargrennan you can climb over the crash barrier by the bridge and walk alongside the quiet River Cree. Spring is a good time for this walk. The peaty water, jostling unhurriedly over rocks, will be canopied with bright new foliage. You'll probably hear cuckoos across the valley and woodpeckers in the woods.

This is a new section of the Southern Upland Way, the result of a spectacularly good idea to realign the long-distance route south following the Cree and then north-west up the Water of Minnoch. The original footpath east of Bargrennan gave walkers a relatively short but unmanageable taste of what it's like in the breadbasket of commercial forestry: swamps and sorrow and sitka spruce.

The waymarked path down the River Cree climbs a little and falls again among trees, eventually emerging at the Clachaneasy Bridge and the back road to Glentrool. Cross the road and continue along the waymarked path. It veers away from the river and arrives at a forest track which you follow for 800 metres, crossing another minor road. Soon you turn right down a waymarked path, heading alongside the Water of Minnoch.

Here, forest management has been handed over to the Cree Valley Community Woodlands Trust. Most of the commercial timber has been removed and the land restocked with native trees. Some inaccessible

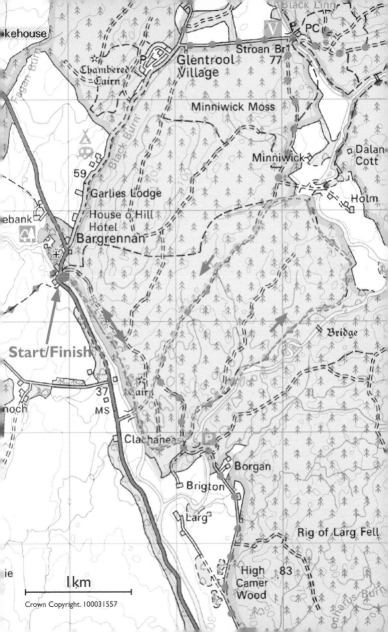

Start/Finish

conifers have even been 'felled to waste'. This term puts a hollow sound in foresters' voices but causes conservationists to grin. Timber left to rot is good for bug life.

The path you follow beside the Minnoch was machine-built in 2001. Reaction to the new route was not universally positive because maps still showed the much shorter original path. Long-distance walkers do not welcome extra miles. Soon after the path was opened I met a coast-to-coaster almost sobbing with rage in the woods. 'Which bureaucratic deviant,' he wanted to know, 'was responsible for this idiotic detour through these bloody bluebell woods?' I sympathised with him, and agreed it was annoying, if he was so far behind schedule; casually taking a moment to zip up my fleece, thus concealing my Countryside Ranger badge.

The machine path intentionally avoids the "Roman Bridge"; a 17th-century crossing of the Water of Minnoch. This simple arch deserves general admiration. The trouble is, it hasn't any parapets. Sanitising the structure for the enjoyment of all is out of the question; you can't add aluminium handrails to a scheduled ancient monument.

Walkers sometimes discover the packhorse bridge by accident. Anyone who visits it is advised not to cross. That doesn't mean they mustn't, it just means everyone's responsible for their own actions. To find the packhorse

Packhorse Bridge

bridge, take a small path off to the right of the Way, just after the second of three wooden footbridges. This takes you past the bridge. Later it connects up with the main path again.

There's a Waymerks kist hidden to the side of the main trail. After that you come to a moss-encrusted dyke and a stone-step stile. Crossing the stile you enter unspoilt ancient woodland.

Waymerks kist

After the path was opened, the Galloway Hill Walkers warned us that the area flooded about once every ten years. Well, that was hard to imagine; the grass was growing on the new path, the tree seedlings were taking root, short-eared owls hunted across acres of former sitka forest. This was paradise on a small scale. As for the river: a more tranquil, acquiescent watercourse it would be hard to imagine.

Then came the winter of 2003. It didn't stop raining for a week. Everything went under water. With a 600 square kilometre catchment, nothing is sacred to the Cree. Even the main Girvan road was submerged.

We didn't lose the path, but some of it got redistributed. A lot of culverts were dislodged too, and had to be replaced by bridges, which cope better. In particular, a large-bore, expensive plastic pipe disappeared completely and is probably still floating around in the Solway. Black and about the size of a well-fed shark, it's capable of causing palpitations in the hearts of bathers.

Climbing through the woods you come out of the flood zone. The remains of dwellings and what may be a corn-drying kiln can be found among the trees. Just before the Holm, turn left at a T-junction in the path, ignoring the arrow pointing right for the Southern Upland Way. This path takes you to a minor road. Turning left again, march south to Clachaneasy Bridge, then right, returning up the Way to Bargrennan.

Don't attempt this walk if, when you get to Bargrennan, the river is in spate. The path will be impassable. During floods, through-walkers are advised to use the road as far as the now redundant Caldons Campsite, just to the west of Loch Trool.

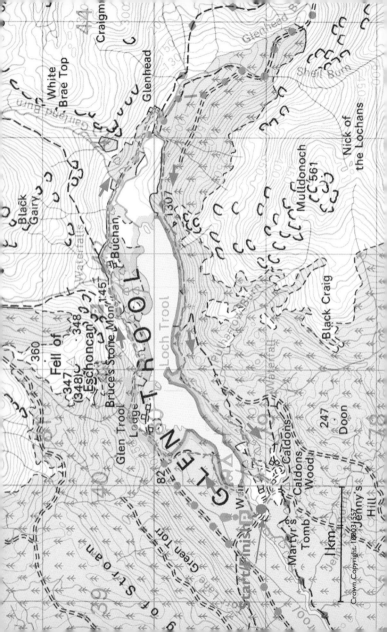

LOCH TROOL

Distance	8.5km (5.5 miles) circular.
Start and Finish	Caldons car park. Turn off the A714 Girvan road at Bargrennan, heading north-east. At Glentrool village turn right just after the houses, signposted for Loch Trool and Bruce's Stone. Keep going, crossing a bridge beside the Visitor Centre and down through mixed woodland until you reach a flat, straight road almost at loch level. Turn right to find the car park by a bridge which crosses the Water of Trool.
Terrain	Woodland track, public road, machine-built path. Boots or strong shoes recommended.
Map	OS Outdoor Leisure 32, Galloway Forest Park or OS Explorer 319.
Refreshments	Stroan Bridge Forestry Commission Visitor Centre (Easter–October: 10.30–16.00) or House o' the Hill Hotel at Bargrennan.

Leave your car in the parking area at the entrance of what used to be Caldons Campsite and head out along a footpath beside the river. This winds through the woods, crosses a small burn and meets the public road. Turn right, past the end of the drive to Glen Trool Lodge, continuing uphill among rhododendrons.

Anyone who has spent time on a rhododendron task force will shudder to look on these glossy-leafed, suckering plants. They're fine in back gardens, briefly glorious in flower. Left to their own devices they rapidly colonise wild places, forming dense, impenetrable forest. Parts of Galloway have become overrun by them. No other plant can compete—the dense, waxy foliage shades out all native species and the leaf litter slowly adapts the soil, making it more and more rhodie-friendly.

There are two car parks near the top of the hill, from which you can start the Merrick climb or head for Buchan Hill. A few metres off the road to the right is a great viewpoint looking across the huge Glenhead basin to the Rig of the Jarkness. Bruce's Stone is here, not quite making it as an aesthetic addition to the landscape. In fact, from some angles it looks a bit like a desktop computer sitting incongruously on a pile of stones. This monument commemorates Robert the Bruce's victory against the English in Scotland's 13th-century struggle for independence. Bruce was able to make good public relations mileage out of it, with the particular nature of the English defeat firing the enthusiasm of fence-sitting nobles.

Cross a narrow stone bridge near Buchan House. An army tank, lost and benighted on exercise, stuck here a few years back and you can still see the scrapes in the stonework.

The track falls away again after Buchan House, descending almost to loch level among fine woods of mature oak. It then crosses the Gairland Burn and approaches Glenhead Farm, the most remote dwelling this side of the Galloway Hills. Before you get to the farm, turn right down a small path, labelled 'Forest Walk' on the side of a ceramic drinking trough. Cross the bridge over the Glenhead Burn and follow the Southern Upland Way uphill as it turns right to go round the south side of the loch.

At the Steps of Trool, two flights of wooden stairs descend a steep slope. These have nothing to do with the name but were the only way to sort out a difficult section of path. This is where the battle took place. A first-rate information panel describing the action and an S-shaped bridge mark the site.

In 1307 an English force under Sir Aymer de Vallance, Earl of Pembroke, tracked a small party of Scots along the south shore of the loch. Pembroke probably thought of it as part of a mopping-up operation after he had defeated Bruce at Methven the previous year. As he gained on the struggling Scots, he didn't realised that most of Bruce's army were hidden on the boulder-strewn slopes above. Timed to perfection, the Scots suddenly emerged from cover, rolling half a hillside of rocks onto the English force and knocking them into the loch. It was a rout, and paved the way for a more decisive Scottish victory at Bannockburn in 1314.

The path climbs and falls along the loch side, much improved by the careful removal of non-native conifers. The views get better all the time. To the north the Fell of Eschoncan and Buchan Hill stand either side of the entrance to a hanging valley. The Buchan Burn falls 200 metres down the hillside with a continuous roar, and the massive bulk of Benyellary takes up sky space behind. Fur-

Fell of Eschoncan

ther east the Gairland Burn, descending from hidden Loch Valley, tumbles white over rocks.

Towards the west end of the loch, follow the path through mature larches. Eventually you descend to a wilderness of unmown grass, the electric points and areas of hard standing the only reminders that this was once the busy campsite of Caldons.

Don't hang around too long here, especially if it is summer, overcast and still. If you do you will be attacked by hordes of tiny black flies—Caldons is Midge Mecca. Few campers who spent a summer's night here ever returned. Instead they dined out on the experience, until even in far corners of the world the name 'Caldons' became associated with insect mayhem.

The campsite finally closed to business in 2004. Various official reasons were offered for this capitulation: the grass cost a lot to cut; repeat business was down. No one said, 'We've got to close it, there just aren't enough masochists to go round.'

Across the bridges and past the information shelter, the haven of your car is just the other side of the Water of Trool.

Over page: The Buchan Burn

WALK 6

27

THE MERRICK

Distance	16km (10 miles) circular.
Start and Finish	Bruce's Stone car park. Turn off the A714 Girvan road at Bargrennan, heading north-east. At Glentrool village turn right just after the houses, signposted for Loch Trool and Bruce's Stone.
Terrain	A complete variety between excellent purpose-built hill path and boggy hole. Take waterproof and windproof clothing, map and compass, and food and drink.
Map	OS Outdoor Leisure 32, Galloway Forest Park or OS Explorer 318.
Refreshments	Stroan Bridge Forestry Commission Visitor Centre (open Easter–October: 10.30–16.00) or House o' the Hill Hotel at Bargrennan

Favouritism, something tells me, has no place in a walks book. I'll have to be careful what I say about the Merrick, emphasising some of its faults.

For one thing, it is often extremely busy. The hill's popularity means conditions underfoot can get tricky after a wet spell. Unlike a lot of the walks in this book, you're almost guaranteed to meet other hikers, unless the weather's rubbish or it's Cup Final day. For me, too many greetings per hour and the hills lose some of their solitude appeal.

To avoid a stampede and yet see the Merrick at its best, choose a day with a cloudless forecast but start as early in the morning as light will allow, walking the hill as a clockwise circuit. This way you'll hardly meet a soul and have allowed maximum margin for error, especially during the winter when the walk will use up a fair proportion of the daylight hours available.

The other thing to consider about the Merrick is its remoteness. While it's not the longest walk in this book, it's probably the one which will take you furthest from civilisation. You don't want to be on Redstone Rig, watching an ominous cloud approaching, only to look in your pack and find you forgot your waterproofs. Or your compass, for that matter. It's worth a few minutes extra, before starting, checking through the contents of your rucksack.

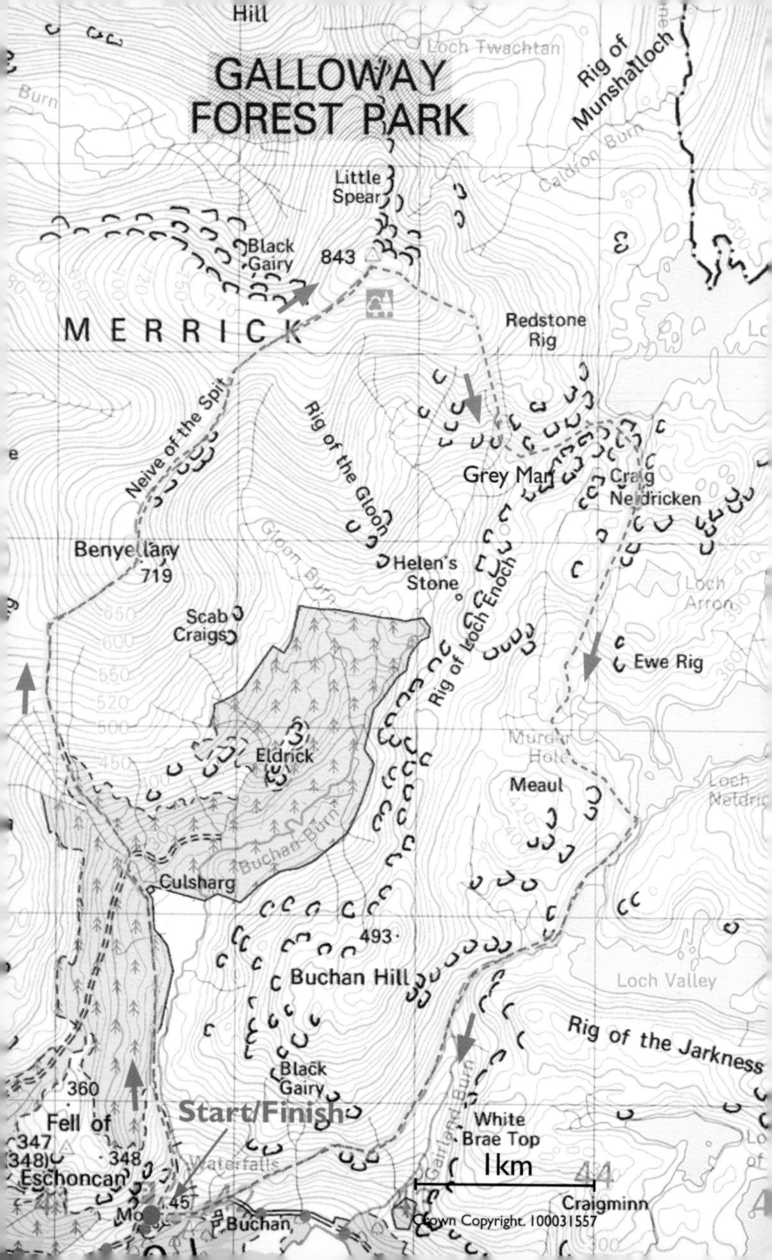

Hill

GALLOWAY
FOREST PARK

Loch Twachtan

Rig of
Munshalloch

Caldron Burn

Little
Spear

Black
Gairy   843

Redstone
Rig

M E R R I C K

Neive of the Spit

Rig of the Gloon

Grey Man

Craig
Neldricken

Benyellary
719

Gloon Burn

Helen's
Stone

Loch
Arron

Scab
Craigs

650
600
550
520
500

Rig of Loch Enoch

Ewe Rig

Eldrick

Murder
Hole

Meaul

Loch
Neldric

Buchan Burn

Culsharg

493

Loch Valley

Buchan Hill

Black
Gairy

Rig of the Jarkness

Start/Finish

360

Garland Burn

White
Brae Top

Fell of
347   Eschoncan
348   348

1km

44

Craigminn

Waterfalls

45

Mo

Buchan

Loch Neldricken and the Merrick

From the upper Bruces's Stone car park, take the boulder-strewn path starting at the Merrick information board, following it up through planted conifers to Culsharg bothy, above which the ascent becomes steeper. Jink right across the forest road and just carry on up. This is the hard graft of the Merrick climb. Among the trees there's less wind to cool your brow or views to ameliorate the slog. In the summer months the heavy smell of pine sap fills the nostrils.

The main climb now is to the top of Benyellery, the name derived from Gaelic 'hill of the eagles'. You can see Ailsa Craig, the volcanic plug sticking up in the Firth of Clyde. Beyond that, the lumpy skyline of Arran culminates in Goatfell, 75km to the northwest. Follow the dyke along the Neive of the Spit and make the final ascent to the Merrick's summit.

A low wall of stones surrounds the trig pillar. As you approach, a couple of heads might pop up suddenly to greet you, and in the lee of that shelter healthless energy foods are shared ravenously among complete strangers.

The view includes the Isle of Man, the coast of Northern Ireland and the hump-backed horizon of the Lake District. The long spur of the Rhins of Galloway stretches out into the sea, crisp and sharp. Loch Doon lies to the north. You get five seconds to take all this in, after that your eyes are watering so much you can hardly see. The wind howls across the hill top, singing in chinks among the stones. If the weather isn't holding up and you need a quick descent, simply retrace your steps. Alternatively, Redstone Rig provides a way off to the south-east, pointing towards Loch Enoch.

To visit the Grey Man of Merrick (NX437 846) you need to come off on the right side of this shoulder, descending to the right of a small burn and heading for the line of a tumbled dyke at the bottom. When the burn reaches flatter ground cross it, turning left round a rocky headland and the Grey Man's profile shows up in the cliff face, best appreciated from the Loch Enoch side.

Continue north-east along a fence, topping a slight rise and overlooking the island-filled Loch Enoch. One of the islands has a loch of its own. The heather-clad eminence to the north is Mullwharchar, meaning 'hill of the huntsman's horn'. A plan to fill this mountain with nuclear waste seems to have been abandoned. I'm glad. Whatever assurances to the contrary, and irrespective of local job-creation sweeteners, I doubt the service roads and subsidiary works for this scheme could be provided without spoiling the wilderness.

Grey Man of Merrick

At the loch's edge you can pass the end of the fence on the beach. Skirting the shore the path turns right. Soon you pick up a burn flowing south, which you'll be following in one form or another all the way down to Glentrool.

The path passes Loch Arron and arrives at the Murder Hole, described in S.R. Crockett's novel *The Raiders*. This small bay at the west end of Loch Neldricken is the fictional site of numerous murders and is said to be frost-resistant. Perhaps a positive correlation exists between homicidal drowning and water temperature. In summer, the high-pitched whine of millions of insects penetrates the silence. Quiet wavelets lap against rocks.

The lochs path is a squelch, even during a drought, but having experienced the windswept summit of the Merrick and the vastness of its surroundings, descending past the lochs provides the perfect contrast. Here it is just as lonely, and yet the limits have come crowding in, intensifying awareness of detail: small sheltered hollows trap the sun. Lizards scuttle. There is the clean, almost briny smell of upland lochs—probably bog myrtle and thyme. Surface ripples fall through feet of clear water to spangle smooth white sand. Turning to look at the sunbathed hump of the mountain you've left behind, it's hard to believe it was so cold up there, or so wind-blasted. Down by the lochs there's a flat calm.

If anywhere in Britain remains untouched by industry, these upland lochs are surely the place? Wrong. They've been exploited. The raw material? Sand. A stick coated in special tar was rolled in it, creating an effective grinding tool. Decades of Sunday roasts throughout Britain were carved with knives sharpened on Merrick sand. Of course, rival sands were available. Cheaper abrasives could be purchased, which would spray their inferior surface material over tablecloths and add crunch to vegetables. But if you wanted the genuine article, super-rough granite sand from these lochs was needed. Like anything else hard to get, it came at a price.

Follow the Mid Burn to Loch Valley which empties down the Gairland Burn. The path eventually rises above this, contouring the shoulder of Buchan Hill, then descends through fields to the forest track in Glentrool. A right turn here takes you back to the car park.

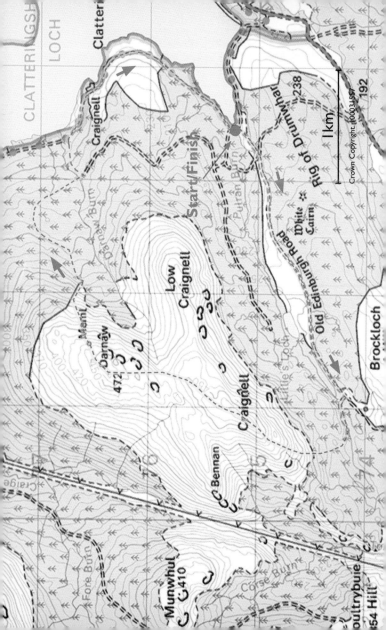

CRAIGNELL AND DARNAW

Distance	10.5km (6.5 miles) circular.
Start and Finish	A parking space beside the road at the southwest tip of Clatteringshaws Loch. Follow the A712 Queen's Way west from New Galloway, pass Clatteringshaws Visitor Centre and drop down beneath the dam, taking a right turn shortly afterwards along a signposted road towards Loch Dee. Cross a narrow bridge at the end of the dam wall and go a further half-mile (800m) to the tip of the loch. You'll know if you've got the right place—there's a green FC footpath sign saying 'Lillie's Loch'.
Terrain	Public road, forest track, steep unmarked hillside, heather upland, forest ride. Boots recommended.
Map	OS Outdoor Leisure 32, Galloway Forest Park or OS Explorer 319.
Refreshments	Clatteringshaws Forestry Commission Visitor Centre. There is a parking fee.
Opening Hours	Easter–October: 10.30–16.00

Craignell and Darnaw are not the easiest of hills to get on and off. They're not particularly high or steep. Nor is there a massive distance involved. It's just that commercial forest surrounds them. You have to take the rough with the smooth. But when you're on the tops, you know that the access difficulties have all been worthwhile.

The Old Edinburgh Road takes you the first stretch. This once important highway used to be the main road between Newton Stewart and Edinburgh. From the village of Minnigaff you can trace it all the way to Clatteringshaws, where it crossed the old stone bridge below the dam, and on to New Galloway over the Ken Bridge. Then it went north to Dalry where it runs up through Craighead. As far as Lillie's Loch it looks just like any other forest road but it's nice to know this was the line followed by centuries of Galloway's travellers. The prodigious hills rising to the north were the companion of their foot-slogged miles too.

Continue beyond the loch until you come to an old quarry, out of which turn right down a small, half-concealed spur of track. This peters out after a few hundred metres, becoming a forest ride. Soon take another right at a multiple ride junction. You'll know if you've made the correct choice as this ride climbs steeply, spruce on one side, larch on the other until it breaks out onto the hillside among bracken. Follow a small watercourse, cross a derelict fence and head for the top.

The steep ascent and rough going through heather are rewarded by stupendous views to the nearest big hills of Drigmorn, Millfore and Cairngarroch. As you gain the summit cairn of Craignell the openness spreads in every direction. If anything could turn a buzzard agoraphobic, Craignell top might do it.

Between you and Darnaw lies a beautiful, rugged, post-glacial upland with striated rock outcrops and massive perched boulders. Small gouged lochans of clear water reflect the sky. Below these ice-hammered heights the softer forests fall away all around. Be sure not to head for Low Craignell—it looks tempting. The bigger hill further north is the one you want. Reaching it means losing a little height, skirting lochans and treading soft moss beds. Cross another dead fence, then climb to Darnaw summit.

About 400 metres to the north-east is a plane-crash memorial. To find it, head directly for Clatteringshaws Loch. The white cottage of Upper Craigenbay on the far side acts as a convenient marker. Descend slightly between two spurs of higher ground until the slope increases. The memorial stands out well if the visibility is good.

This is where the *Daily Express* Dragonfly crashed in the winter of

The Dragonfly crash memorial

Looking towards Low Craignell and Clatteringshaws

1937. Its disappearance caused a massive air search, but it was a local shepherd who eventually discovered the burnt out wreckage, tail-plane pointing skyward. Poor weather, high ground and low-tech flight are an unhealthy combination, tending to result in what accident investigators euphemistically call CFIT—Controlled Flight Into Terrain. Seventy years on, droplets of melted aluminium lie among the stones. All four airmen, who were surveying routes for night-flight airmail services, died here. It's not a morbid place, to my mind. There are surely worse deaths than running smack into Darnaw—it beats most for drama and brevity.

From the memorial, continue in a straight line downhill to a dyke which separates open hill from forest plantation. Turn right until you come to a break in the trees. Here you can follow the dyke downhill, heading for a large area of clearfell and younger trees, your first objective being the forest track at the bottom. Don't be tempted to descend all the way down the Darnaw Burn; it's a real scramble and will take you twice as long. Instead, keep to the left side of the clearfell/second rotation forestry, cross the dyke and follow the edge of the standing crop down hill. This is actually a purpose-built route for forest rangers' quad bikes and gives easy walking. A few metres down there's a massive, heather-topped boulder.

Once you hit the forest track turn right for 300 metres, then left down the Darnaw Burn. There's a derelict fence and tumbled dyke to cross. Take the right hand side of the burn and follow it another 300 metres down to the road.

If for some reason you can't get down the Darnaw Burn, you could find your car by continuing along the forest track. The trouble is, there are first a ranger's sighting range and second an active road-stone quarry. Getting shot and then blasted, though dramatic and brief, are not the way to end a good walk. Besides, excellent views over Clatteringshaws Loch are missed if you stay in the forest. Better brave the dubious-looking ride down the burn. Once on the single-track road from Craigencallie, turn right and skirt the lochside past Craignell Farm to your car.

And if you're suffering from calorific shortfall, the Clatteringshaws Visitor Centre is just round the corner.

Bog myrtle on the side of Clatteringshaws Loch

ST JOHN'S TOWN OF DALRY

Distance	4.5km (3 miles) circular.
Start and Finish	By Dalry town hall (where there are toilets). Park anywhere on the High Street. Dalry is on the A713, 25km/16 miles north-west of Castle Douglas.
Terrain	Grazed meadows and hillside, public road and waymarked path. Boots or strong shoes recommended.
Map	OS Outdoor Leisure 32, Galloway Forest Park, or OS Explorer 318.
Refreshments	Reasonable choice in Dalry.
Other Interests	You may see Red Kites; over 100 birds have been reintroduced to the area in the last few years.

The placename Dalry simply means 'King's meadow'. St John's connection with the village is harder to fathom. At the top end of the main street, by the Southern Upland Way fingerpost, a low stone seat called St John's Chair is positioned against a wall. But John the Baptist certainly never came near it. He wouldn't have wanted to, either—it's a most uncomfortable-looking seat.

The township's name is more probably derived from a dedication awarded to the local church by the Knights Templar, some time after 1118. Protecting the interests of pilgrims resulted in the establishment of routes and hostels to cater for through traffic. On the busy trail between Edinburgh and St Ninian's shrine at Whithorn, Dalry catered for droves of travellers headed for sacred places, among them King James IV in 1497. He paid eighteen shillings (90p) for bed and breakfast and five shillings (25p) for his party to cross the Water of Ken by ferryboat.

Take the footpath beside the village hall. It descends between the church and a Norman motte. Mottes were feudal powerbases, consisting of improved and fortified hillocks, which now have the appearance of upturned pudding basins. Cross the Water of Ken on the suspension bridge and turn left down a flight of steps, following the path through fields to the road. Turn right for a short distance, then left, rejoining the Southern Upland Way by the salmon ladder at Earlstoun Power Station.

WALK 9

Galloway's hydro-electric scheme must be one of the greatest hydrological embezzlements of all time: disregarding natural watersheds, it steals water from all over the place. Rain falling on north-facing slopes makes for the Clyde but is piped back south to augment the natural flow of the Water of Deugh. As for the Black Water of Dee, its resources are trapped by Clatteringshaws Dam and brought 6km underground to drive the turbines at Glenlee. You can see the pipe as you walk along. It descends the wooded slope of Black Bank to the south-west.

Leave the Southern Upland Way, climbing Waterside Hill beside the dyke until you come beyond a sheep pen. You are following in the footsteps of Adam Forrester and, indirectly, of Robert Burns' better known Tam o' Shanter. Both, on their drunken way home from the pub, witnessed a witch's coven dancing. Forrester, peering through the windows of Dalry church, recognised his favourite barmaid partnering the devil and unthinkingly shouted 'Ye'll no deny this the morn.' The witches came after him. With his horse exhausted by the chase, Forrester dismounted and drew a circle on the ground with his

Looking down into the Garroch Glen

WALK 9

sword, defying evil to enter it in the name of God.

Robert Burns probably heard this story locally before writing Tam o' Shanter, though he sets his tale in Ayrshire. Tam's story stops at the river, where Burns makes use of the adage that witches can't cross running water. Dalry's witches had no such scruples.

Adam Forrester's Circle, or the Witch's Scour, still exists near the top of Waterside Hill. Contour the slope until you come to a hawthorn. Turn left and head towards the

Covenanter's grave

dyke at the bottom of the hill. Keep to the drier ground, skirt an area of bracken and find a small outcrop of rock, perhaps 200 metres short of the dyke. Then walk 35 paces back towards Dalry and you should come across a circular trench in the turf. If it's rained recently it will be full of water and show up fine.

In the 19th century, grid ref NX 606817 became the focus of a popular pilgrimage. The link between Adam Forrester's Circle and Burns' poem sparked the public imagination. Special excursions were arranged, bringing parties of sightseers from the Central Belt.

Return to Dalry by rejoining the Southern Upland Way via the top of Waterside Hill. There are great views down the Garroch Glen and over to the Rhins of Kells. Keep on the trail all the way back to the Water of Ken suspension bridge. Opposite the information shelter a stone stile gives access to the churchyard where, in the corner nearest the bridge, a covenanter's grave stands.

During the Killing Times of 1684-85, Scottish Presbyterians were routinely hunted down in remote places of worship and shot. The hills of Dumfries and Galloway are littered with the graves of covenanting martyrs. Near to Dalry school stands a tree-like memorial, and you can read about the troubles. It seems a shame those 17th-century Christians couldn't simply rejoice in the similarity of their beliefs, instead of shooting each other to bits in out-of-the-way places.

With luck your return to the village will neatly coincide with the pubs starting to serve lunch.

Earlstoun power station

Mon

Skeoch Hill

Skeoch

Three

Midtown

250

220

Cornlee Hill

Scaur Fm

Glenkiln 133

Glenkiln Reservoir

Glenkiln

Sculptures

Start/Finish

Cornlee

6

Stone

5

Sculptures

1

3

Sculptures

4

158

Margreig

Glenkiln Hill

Shiel Head

Bennan

226

Sculptures

2

Shalloch

1km

Crown Copyright. 100031557

1. John the Baptist, Auguste Rodin
2. Standing Figure, Henry Moore
3. Glenkiln Cross, Henry Moore
4. Visitation, Jacob Epstein
5. Two Piece Reclining Figure No. 1, Henry Moore
6 King and Queen, Henry Moore

8

ner's ument

GLENKILN

Distance	6.5km (4 miles) circular.
Start and Finish	Car park at the northwest end of Glenkiln Reservoir. Turn off the A75 signposted for Shawhead, about 10km/6 miles west of Dumfries. In the village, turn right, then left, following signs for Dunscore, then left again signposted Glenkiln.
Terrain	Public road, grazed hillside, farm track. Boots or strong shoes recommended.
Map	OS Explorer 321, Nithsdale and Dumfries.
Refreshments	Nothing in the immediate area. Take a flask and a snack.

Sculptures aside, our countryside is full of stuff. A century ago, before electricity, there would hardly have been anything out there at all. Now almost every hilltop has something on it: a TV relay cluster, a mobile phone mast, a radar station. The glens and vales, pylon-studded, have become convenient ducts, carrying essential high-voltage cables from place to place. All the gadgets of the modern age adorned Scotland's great outdoors, even before the forests of wind turbines began to appear in the 1990s.

Where does countryside sculpture fit in? Art in the countryside often gets a rough ride: 'We don't want that thing stuck on that hill!' Sometimes, failing to see the purpose in sculpture, I am inclined to agree. But considering all the other stuff foisted on our green places, does it matter? A visit to Glenkiln, 13km west of Dumfries, is almost guaranteed to produce a reaction.

The Glenkiln sculptures were bought by the landowner, Tony Keswick, and controversially positioned by the reservoir in the 1950s. To take a walking tour of them, start at Auguste Rodin's bronze interpretation of John the Baptist, beside the Marglolly Burn. This is the best place to leave your car. Turn right out of the car park to see 'Standing Figure' by Henry Moore. Then retrace your steps along the road to a rather overgrown gate on the right, from which you can climb steeply to the Glenkiln Cross, part of Moore's crucifixion triptych. The cross stands alone here at a good viewpoint. If the wind direction is right the bronze vibrates slightly, making a small singing sound.

From the cross, head south-east, roughly in the direction of Criffel, and pass through a farm gate, fastened with baler twine. Having passed through, try replicating the knot used by the farmer—baler twine is itself a sophisticated countryside art-form. If you continue in a straight line, passing between two conifer plantations, you come to the next sculpture. However, the going is rough and wet and you're just as well veering left before the plantations. Drop down to a vehicle track and turn right. Then, a few hundred metres along, look for a small stand of Scots pine on the left. In among the trees is 'Visitation' by Sir Jacob Epstein.

Continuing along the track you eventually meet the public road. Turn hard left, descending on tarmac to Henry Moore's 'Two Piece Reclining Figure No. 1'. Originally cast in bronze, this was withdrawn from the collection, then replaced by a bronze-dust impregnated glass-fibre replica. Nearby Morrinton Quarry supplied the ten-tonne stone for it to sit on.

Further down the road, go left at a junction beside a topiary bird and climb again past the dam. Just beyond the gate leading to some sheds, another gate gives access up on your left. Having kept the best till last, climb the sloping field to Moore's 'King and Queen'. Then return to your car, dropping back to the road again on a track running to the left.

In terms of communication, sculpture is not so different from most of the other stuff spiking the tops of hills. But we could speculate for many pages on just why sculpture communicates, and what it communicates to the individual. In ignorance of anything unusual about Glenkiln, I first

'King and Queen'

drove along the side of the reservoir in 1987 and, happening to glance up, saw what I took to be two shepherds on the hillside. They turned out to be a sculptured man and woman, the 'King and Queen'.

Still unenlightened, I later came across a spooky woman in a wood. I drew my own conclusions: this was a bronze representation of a pregnant, tubercular female, probably a 19th-century workhouse escapee. Perhaps she told a true story. She looked in poor shape to me; clinging

'Visitation'

to life by a thread. I felt sympathetic. Actually this was 'Visitation', Epstein's depiction of the Virgin Mary.

Graffiti appears on 'Two Piece Reclining Figure' from time to time and in 1995 the heads of Moore's 'King and Queen' were removed by vandals, exhibiting an even less sophisticated reaction to art. The royal heads were eventually traced to London and seamlessly restored to necks.

A walk around Glenkiln's sculpture collection takes no more than a couple of hours. The images it leaves in the mind are durable, taking time to digest.

And as Henry Moore said: 'Sculpture should always at first have some obscurities and further meanings. People should want to go on looking and thinking; it should never tell all about itself immediately.'

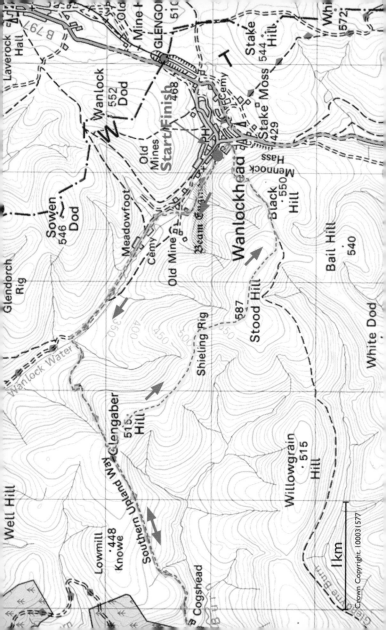

WANLOCKHEAD

Distance	7km (4.5 miles) circular or 10km (6.5 miles) taking in the waymerks kist.
Start and Finish	Wanlockhead Lead Mining Museum car park. Wanlockhead is signposted off the A76, 40km/24 miles north of Dumfries.
Terrain	Grazed hillside, machine-built path with waymarking, path undefined over hills. Boots recommended.
Map	OS Explorer 329, Lowther Hills, Sanquhar & Leadhills.
Refreshments	Shop, tearoom and cafe at the Lead Mining Museum (when open).
Opening Hours	The Lead Mining Museum (entry fee) has displays and very good guided tours underground as well as visits to miners' cottages. Open Easter-Oct: daily 11.00-16.30. (Note: Times change over course of season. The museum's future was uncertain as we went to press so it might be worth checking in advance that it is open.)

The Mennock Pass through the Lowther Hills is like a miniature Glencoe. The heather-covered slopes crowd in upon the traveller, spectacular but manageable, not quite as forbidding. Just before the road leaves the floor of the glen it crosses a bridge. Immediately afterwards, on the left, a white cross lies in the turf. This commemorates a district midwife who died here in the 1930s.

Having delivered a baby in Wanlockhead, she set off to cycle home to Sanquhar on her standard-issue, sit-up-and-beg bicycle. People driving past later that day discovered a scattering of rod-and-lever brake parts on the road. Fearing the worst, they followed the trail down until they came upon the midwife. She had negotiated every bend in the lower pass at breakneck speed. A few metres from safety, the left-hander through the bridge unnerved her. She opted instead for a soft-looking grassy bank. That's where you'll find the cross.

Wanlockhead is 422 metres above sea level, making it the highest inhabited village in Scotland. This distinction is offset by a short growing season and an altitude-depressed ambient temperature. The settlement came into being because of lead ore, deep inside the Lowthers.

Lead was mined here during the 13th century, though its discovery is thought to have been in Roman times. Gold was found too, the metal eventually making its way into the Scottish Crown. In between obsessive bouts of gold-panning, lead mining and smelting supported a growing population, reaching its peak in the 19th century. Many of the hills round about are riddled with shafts. One, the New Glencrieff, goes down 460 metres: 120 metres below sea level.

Ore wagons and beam engine

Start by walking north-west from the museum along the Southern Upland Way. You pass a beam engine and various other mining relics along the course of an old narrow-gauge railway. Cross the Wanlock Water and climb the side of Glengaber Hill on a switchback track. This brings you near the summit above a deep gorge. It's a good place to see peregrines.

Behind, the managed heather uplands are a dappled mosaic, achieved by controlled burning. Older heather plants are torched, encouraging new shoots to grow. Red grouse eat the new growth, taking refuge in mature heather nearby. Thus cosseted, they live here in large numbers. You hear their raucous calls from time to time.

Over the glen, on the slopes of Sowen Dod, a whole hillside has been laid bare by an ore-smelting works. Poisonous lead residue sterilises the landscape; nothing much grows, even a hundred years after abandonment.

From the shoulder of Glengaber you can, if you wish, continue along the Southern Upland Way, downhill on a nice grassy path to Cogshead. There is a ruined farmhouse there and a Waymerks kist. In the farmhouse garden a crop of rhubarb is all that remains of the vegetable plot. Rhubarb survives decades of neglect in wild places—sheep can't handle the taste. Returning to the shoulder of Glengaber, leave

View over Wanlockhead from Green Hill

the SUW, turning right just before the stile, climbing first Glengaber Hill and then Stood Hill with the fence on your left.

On a clear day the views are superb. To the north you can see the peaks of the Highlands. I'm reliably informed the Paps of Jura are visible from here, though I've never been able to decide which they are. There are loads of paps over there, any might be them.

Meeting a fence junction, pass through a gate to your left, then another gate on your right gets you out onto Green Hill. Wanlockhead lies below in its sheep-nibbled vale. Above it, on Lowther Hill, the radar station monitors a sky-full of no-frills transatlantic flights. This also marks the Southern Upland Way's highest point at 710 metres. From Green Hill descend to Black Hill. Then take the easy track back into the village.

If your homeward drive is back through the pass, look for a rusty cube beside the Mennock Water. In the 1920s a gang broke into premises in Sanquhar, failed to open the strongbox and so barrowed it outside to their getaway truck. Its weight encouraged them. It felt like coal-miners' wage packets.

They threw it from a bridge, but this failed to break the door. The rest of the night was spent hauling it back to road level. Finally the sweating thieves set off again, taking the Mennock Pass. A fall into the burn seemed just the thing to bust a safe, so they shoved it over. Sure enough, the door flew off before it reached the bottom. Cheering, they scrambled down to collect the swag.

There were no wads of banknotes. The safe's contents amounted to £22 in threepenny pieces, the result of a year's charitable collection on shop counters throughout the district. In the 1970s, after decimalisation, people were still discovering those heavy, brass-coloured coins among the grass. The disgusted thieves never bothered to pick them up.

CLOUD HILL AND WELLTREES TAPPIN

Distance	20km (12.5 miles) circular. This can be shortened to 16km (10 miles) if you miss out the kist at Cloud Hill. Missing out Kemp's Castle as well makes the distance 13.5km (8.5 miles).
Start and Finish	Park anywhere along Sanquhar High Street.
Terrain	Public road, hill track, waymarked path and undefined hill path, rough in places. Boots recommended. Take water-proofs, windproofs, map and compass, food and drink.
Map	OS Explorer 328, Sanquhar & New Cumnock.
Refreshments	Reasonable choice in Sanquhar.
Opening Hours	Sanquhar Tollbooth: Apr-Sept, Tues-Sat 10.00-17.00; Sun 14.00-17.00. Admission free.

An 1860s photograph of Sanquhar High Street shows it very much as it is today. Looking north-west past Britain's oldest post office, the thoroughfare appears to end at the Tolbooth, which forms such an efficient pinch-point it's a wonder anything gets through at all. The townspeople in that early photograph watch the camera quizzically from a safe distance. You can imagine the photographer emerging from beneath the camera's hood, imploring them to adopt natural postures. 'For goodness sake, my man, go about your business,' he tells the labourer in the slouch hat. But all to no avail; having volunteered time to humour a freak, the people of Sanquhar are going to stand and stare at him. You can see on their faces—for them it's almost as good as a public holiday.

Before beginning the walk, have a look round the Tolbooth Museum. The building used to house the gaol, which for a while was so easy to get out of, most inmates were on the town every night making merry. Getting back in again was trickier, especially with a skinful. Eventually, a prisoner slipped and broke a leg, the gaoler finally realised what was going on and boarded up the skylight.

Start the walk by heading south-east along the High Street. Turn right at the edge of town, along the Southern Upland Way, beneath an avenue of trees to the castle. This belonged to William Douglas, first

Duke of Queensbury, in the 17th century. He built a much grander residence at Drumlanrig but only slept a single night there, preferring Sanquhar Castle. Unfortunately the ruins are surrounded by fences. It's as hard to get in for a look around now as when the fortifications were at the cutting edge.

Follow the Southern Upland Way along beside the River Nith. Pass an information shelter and turn left over the Blackaddie road bridge, continuing past Ulzieside Farm (pronounced 'Oolieside') onto the hill. Cross the Whing Burn on a stout footbridge and keep going. It's not a steep climb. You'll see a waymarker ahead and think, 'That must be the top!' No way. Distant posts on the skyline raise your hopes several times before you finally arrive.

At the head of the burn, climb the fence stile, descend over the dyke, and go up again to the top of Cloud Hill. There is a Waymerks kist nearby. You get a magnificent view down the Scar Glen to the south-east, overlooked by its rugged outcrop of rock and scree.

It's easiest to retrace your steps now, re-crossing the stile at the top of the Whing Burn. From there, leave the SUW, climbing gently to Whing Head and then on to Welltrees Tappin with its trig pillar and spectacular views. As far as the eye can see, hills roll away in every direction; it's like being on a wave crest in the middle of an ocean.

Corridow is the next summit, and it lies directly along the dry-stone dyke to the east. Go almost to the plantation's boundary fence before turning north towards Sanquhar. There is a quad-bike track running down the side of the wood which makes for easier going.

The Whing Burn has some juniper beside it, clinging to a crag. The shrub is now a rarity in this part of Scotland, having been grazed out by sheep until it holds on marginally in isolated clumps. However, at the time of writing the Whing is being developed to conserve black grouse. A lot of the blow grass (otherwise known as purple moor grass; the tussock-forming, ecological dead-end stuff which has little nutritional value and is such a pain to walk over) will be discouraged, allowing heather regeneration and, on the burn slopes, native scrubland. Sheep are out of favour. Biodiversity is set to rise.

Cairn Hill is next on your descent. If you stand beside the cairn you can count your steps to find the Devil's Dyke: an ancient earthwork. Head downhill towards Sanquhar. After 300 paces the slope

The Devil's Dyke

lessens and the Dyke runs across your path, roughly west to east, capped by rushes. Sneeze and you'll miss it.

The Royal Commission on Ancient and Historical Monuments describes it to perfection: 'In appearance it is an earthen bank, running irregularly across the brae face, measuring some 8ft broad at base, narrowing upward and some 2ft in height, while the trench has a breadth of about 7ft and is now shallow. Where the bank has been broken by sheep it is shown to be formed with a core of boulders laid horizontally. Here, indeed, it has the appearance of being wholly formed of slabs, generally about 2-3 feet long by 18 inches wide, while in the usual earthy structure the stones are mostly such as may be carried in the hand.'

While the Commission catalogues a monument in exquisite detail, it steadfastly resists the temptation to offer the smallest crumbs of explanation. The expectant reader sits muttering in the reference library. 'What is it? Why was it? When?' No answers. The author sticks to his guns, never committing himself to interpretation.

The Devil's Dyke drops down into the Whing Burn to your left and disappears into the conifer plantation to your right. As a theoretical whole it forms a wide, spurred curve, starting at Loch Ryan near Stranraer and finishing 130km away on the Solway near Annan. Older

OS maps show extant sections of 'Deil's Dyke', calling it by name. Subsequently, the monument lost favour with archaeological schools of thought and no longer appears on the maps.

Make of it what you will. Was it a prehistoric rampart, dividing Dumfries and Galloway into smaller kingdoms, repelling uncouth neighbours? Or are its existing parts merely dissociated remnants of early field boundaries, which have no connection with each other at all, except that they follow general principles of ideology and construction? Whichever you believe, you can't help marvelling at the scale of the earthwork.

Rejoin the SUW to the east of Whing Burn, turning right towards Sanquhar. If you've energy for another monument, take a wicket gate on the left after you've crossed the Euchan Water. Pass the Euchan Well and continue along a brick-edged path to Kemp's Castle. This Iron Age fort takes advantage of two watercourses meeting to occupy an excellent defensible position. On top, a natural plateau has been beautifully levelled and there are subsidiary earthworks to the upstream end. Mature oak trees surround the periphery, where once stood a wooden palisade.

If you're fit for the extra mile, carry on upriver past the falls. The Euchan Water rumbles at the bottom of an impressive gorge. Emerging onto a minor road, turn right and return past the golf course, heading straight for St Bride's church tower. Then follow the green-signposted road option of the Southern Upland Way back into town.

Kemp's Castle

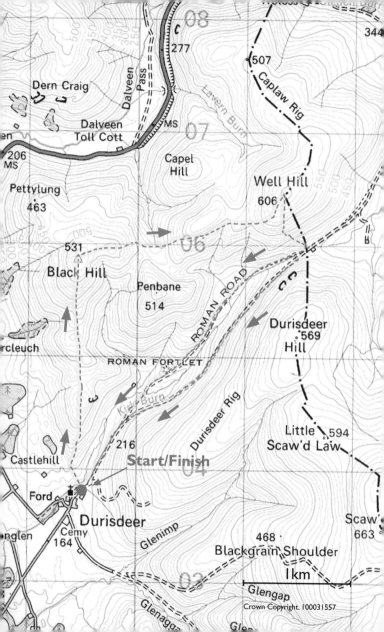

WALK 13
DURISDEER AND WELL HILL

Distance	9km (5.5 miles) circular.
Start and Finish	Park by the war memorial in the centre of Durisdeer. The village is just off the A702 between Carronbridge and Elvanfoot.
Terrain	Steep hill path and grazed upland, farm track, plus some boggy ground. Boots recommended.
Map	OS Explorer 329, Lowther Hills, Sanquhar & Leadhills.
Refreshments	In Sanquhar or Thornhill.
Other Activities	Morton Castle (NX891993) off the A702 south-east of Durisdeer is a fine 14th-century ruin. Drumlanrig Castle, home of the Duke of Buccleuch, is open Apr-Oct for park, gardens and playgrounds, guided tours May-Aug 12.00-16.00.

Durisdeer is a pretty village. Its traditional sandstone houses stand on top of a low hill, arranged around a small square. Two things are especially impressive. The first: the place is exceptionally well-kept. Everything painted has a fresh coat. Everything mown would pass muster for a bowling green. It all points to a serious amount of hard graft.

The other impressive thing is the church. Built in 1699, it takes up one side of the village square with its beautifully proportioned facades. Inside there are two airy galleries and some original box pews. Through a window behind the altar you can see the canopy over the Drumlanrig Dukes' elaborate burial place, the Queensbury Mausoleum. It's a lump of marble, on legs. At the time of manufacture I bet it was considered the height of elegance. Lesser mortals had to make do with churchyard burial; among them is Daniel McMichael, a Covenanter, executed during the Killing Times in 1685.

Having parked by the war memorial, leave the square to the right of the church. At the end of the houses pass through a gate and take another through the dyke on your left, descending to cross the burn at a shallow ford. Then scale ancient earthworks on the side of the bluff and begin the ascent on a red soil sheep path.

The 100 metre climb onto the spur of Wether Hill is unremitting. Turning round at the top, you get the benefit. Durisdeer lies below, almost completely hidden among trees. Beyond it the fertile floodplain

Durisdeer and Penbane

of the Carron Water, and behind that the Nith, delineate the undulating heartland of Drumlanrig Estate. At the back, the range of hills near Moniaive stands up: Cairnkinna, Arkland and Twentyshilling.

Turning again, don't be tempted by Penbane, off to the right—it looks every bit as alluring as Black Hill. Instead of climbing Penbane, your objective is to walk in a circuit round the back of it. Keeping to your original line, drop off the shoulder heading for the mass of Black Hill. Pass through a slip gate beside a redundant sheep pen and up through another gate, following a quad bike track.

It's quite a haul to the summit, but the view from the top is a complete panorama. Lowther Hill with its golf-ball radar station stands to the north. Steygail drops steeply down into the Dalveen Pass. To the east you look across into the hills of South Lanarkshire and to the south lies the whole of Nithsdale. Cloud shadows chase one another across the hills, dappling the silent landscape.

From the trig pillar, head east down over Greentrough Head and into Wee Capel Cleugh before climbing again alongside a fence which rounds the side of Turn Hill. Keep the fence on your left. It meets a slumped dyke which you follow to reach the summit of Well Hill.

The dyke is interesting. After a hundred years or so the heart of a dry-stone wall can start to fall away, allowing the structure to collapse in on itself. In this case the main building stones seem responsible for the failure. The rock appears to be a metamorphic sand or mudstone banded with quartz. It has proved frost-susceptible; the individual stones are falling to bits. Hardly surprising the dyke is mostly on the floor.

At the top of Well Hill only a derelict gate separates you from South Lanarkshire. Turn right. The descent here is steep. Set off at an angle away from the fence but don't follow this bearing all the way to the bottom or you'll come off Wee Well Craigs. About 200 metres down there's a sheep path which heads back to the left, allowing a more reasonable descent. Whatever we assume about the intellectual deficiencies of sheep, they can be relied upon to know the best way off a hill.

Radar station on Lowther Hill, seen from Black Hill top

WALK 13

Once at the bottom there are two options. A quick, dry-footed return to Durisdeer can be made by passing through the gate in the dyke, turning right and following the track down the left side of the Kirk Burn. Alternatively, if you don't mind a bit of swamp-hopping, keep the Well Hill side of the dyke, turn right and pick up the smooth-mounded ancient earthwork of the Well Road running downhill.

Whatever ingenuity the Romans used to cross the poorly drained slopes below Wee Well Craigs has not survived. Occasional bits of the road are visible. Other times you'll be too busy teetering on a tussock to take much notice. This sounds off-putting but the bonus of taking this more difficult path lies below Dash Cleugh. It's an extant Roman fortlet—a complete and unblemished earthwork. This hand-dug trench-and-mound profile, topped by wooden barricades, provided garrison accommodation. It would have been infinitely preferable to camping beside the road in the wild hills around Durisdeer.

A little beyond the fort you can cross the burn and the dyke, soon meeting the main hill track running back down into the village.

Fertile meadow under Well Hill

OAKRIGG TO CAT SHOULDER

Distance	The full circuit is 25km (16 miles) and is a grand day out if you're feeling fit and the weather's good. A shorter version of 12.5km (8 miles) can easily be achieved by starting at Craig-beck Bridge. Alternatively, Oakrigg, Dumcrieff and French-land Tower make an excellent circular walk of 8km (5 miles) in their own right, beginning in the town centre.
Start and Finish	Park in the centre of Moffat (or at Craigbeck Bridge, reached by car 2km/1.5 miles along the Selkirk Road out of Moffat, then turning sharp right down the minor road opposite a timber lorry turning circuit).
Terrain	Public road, forest track and waymarked hill trail, undefined over grazed farmland. Boots recommended. For the longer options, take with you waterproofs, windproofs, map, compass and food and drink.
Map	OS Explorer 330, Moffat & St Mary's Loch. This covers most of the route, though not the southernmost extremities.
Refreshments	Wide choice in Moffat. You may wish to stock up on Moffat Toffees before you start this one.

From the town centre walk up Well Street, cross the Birnock Water footbridge and veer right to meet the Selkirk road running out of town. Turn south along Old Carlisle Road past quality accommodation. Many of these houses were once schools; Moffat was renowned as a centre for educational excellence.

After 800 metres, bear right at a Y-junction. Another 800 metres brings you to the Southern Upland Way. Head east, making the short steep climb onto Oakrigg. From the top there are good views west over the Annan and Evan Valleys. If you've a decent pair of binoculars you can pick out Lochhouse Tower (beside the A701, between the motorway and Moffat). It was built by the Johnstones in the 16th century. Only the wealthiest families could afford this style of protection from the lawlessness of the Border country. The Johnstones, however, seemed to have felt the pinch during construction; they saved money by building rounded corners to their tower, rather than go to the extra expense of using faced cornerstones.

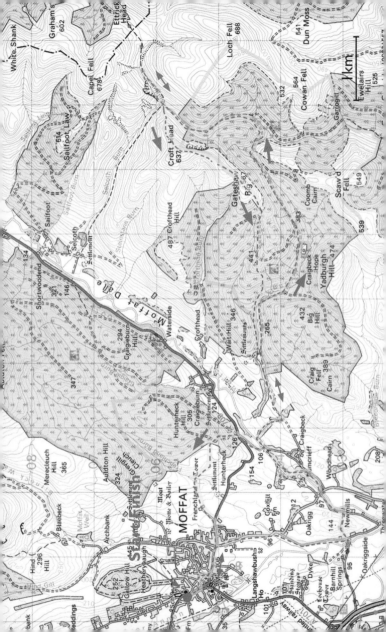

To the east, the Georgian mansion among woodland is Dumcrieff, 1787 residence of John Loudon McAdam, the road surfacing pioneer. Three thousand years before the invention of tarmac, Dumcrieff had a small fort, the name stemming from the Gaelic dun craobh 'fort among trees'.

Staying on the national trail, drop down to the road, pass the entrance to Dumcrieff and enter the finest beech wood in Annandale, planted around the time the house was built. The 250-year-old trees are at their magnificent best. Beyond the wood you come to lush riverside meadows, dotted with Dumcrieff's parkland trees.

Follow Southern Upland Way markers for the next 5km. A farm road becomes a woodland track, climbing steeply through forestry, past isolated Craigbeck Hope cottage and areas of clear-felled spruce. Relics of earlier land use have become exposed by timber harvesting: sheep pens, sheds and dipping trough, all until recently forgotten among trees. The forest road hairpins, heading for derelict Garrogill Farm, but you need to turn left, still with the national trail, following a rocky path up the Wamphray Burn.

Moffat District's postal rounds took in Garrogill until it became vacant in the 1950s. The postman, issued with a bicycle, was expected to deliver mail to three remote farms before returning to the sorting office. These hillsides weren't planted then. There was no forest road. The only way was on foot, but when those distant deliveries were accomplished, the day's work was done. The postman would retrieve his bicycle from the hedge near Craigbeck and ride back into town.

The Wamphray Burn's moss-crusted screes give way to heather and the path emerges into the open near the burn's source. On your left the steep flank of Crofthead towers against the sky and ahead is the exposed crag of Craigmichen Scar. You can follow the Way a little beyond it, if you wish. The Selcoth Burn roars unseen at the bottom—Selcoth, from the Gaelic, meaning 'awesome', or from old Scots meaning 'strange, rare'. After a cairn the path descends, crossing the water on the Gorilla's Bridge. This was built in 2006 to replace the original, which got over-washed with boulders during a storm. Unable to finance helicopter transport for large components, the ranger service devised a sectional steel span. Every stick,

WALK 14

Selcoth Burn and sheep

including half a tonne of foundation concrete, was hand-delivered from the cairn—a project with which the 1950s Moffat postman might have sympathised.

After the sweat of installation, we were inordinately proud of this bridge. Once, while I stood admiring it, a walker appeared. 'You must've hired a team of gorillas to carry that in,' he said. Unsure if this was a compliment, I couldn't immediately decide how to reply. Climbing up the bridge and stumbling slightly as he descended, the walker shouted back, 'You need to be a damn gorilla to get over it an' all.' There's a Waymerks kist close by.

Return to the sheep stell. This was repaired during 2004, at which time the dyker discovered a date-stone recording its original construction by RA in 1787. RA wrote his name twice on the same stone, keen to personalise his workmanship, but then used it as a throughstane, secreted deep in the body of the dyke.

Immediately ahead of you is Cat Shoulder. Don't tackle this climb in rain, snow, ice, low cloud, or if you suffer from vertigo—simply return the way you came. You'll go ass over tip if you miss a step on Cat Shoulder—that phrase refers, of course, to the difficulty even pack mules experience on such slopes. At the time of writing, the most ambitious path project the Southern Upland Way has ever seen (and it's seen a few) was still no more than a twinkle in a ranger's eye. Can the national trail be re-routed via Cat Shoulder?

If you climb you can reach Crofthead (637 metres) and miss out repeat miles of forest road. The views from the top are superb. Criffel rises beside the silver sheet of the Solway Firth, 65km away. Burnswark stands out—a flat-topped hill fort adapted for training by the Romans. To the north, the Selkirk road runs into the Scottish Borders and the big Moffat hills stand up above the dale: Saddle Yoke, White Coomb and Hart Fell.

Head south-west, keeping close to the fence along Crookedside Schlenders, descending Gateshaw Rig. Turn left at the forest road and eventually right, down a purpose-built zig-zag path called Dry Gutter. Path building of this sort is a highly specialised skill, especially on severe slopes, where the drainage is critical.

Follow this pending re-alignment of the Southern Upland Way along a short stretch of forest road, through an area of clearfell, then down through deep dark sitka forest until you cross the Cornel Burn, rejoining the original route at the forest edge.

Return to Moffat the way you came. Alternatively, leave the national trail at Craigbeck Bridge, cross the Selkirk road and climb Hunterheck Hill's forest track. After 500 metres, a break on the left allows access to fields above Frenchland. The way to this 16th-century tower house can be boggy and overgrown. Moreover, you'll need to hop over the Frenchland Burn. It's a scramble.

Frenchland Tower is a ruin. Corbelling at the top of the west wall once supported a walkway, desirable if it pleased you to drop things on the heads of unwanted visitors. By the time the extension was added to hold an improved staircase, defence had become less important, hence the low window in the south wall. Domestic arrangements (like the salt-keep beside a first floor fireplace) can

WALK 14

Frenchland Tower

be seen from inside, but as this building isn't maintained for sight-seeing it's best not to loiter for fear of falling masonry.

Head towards Moffat across the field, meeting a track through steadings. This takes you back to the Selkirk road. Turn right and leg it for the nearest teashop.

LANGHOLM AND POTHOLM

Distance	9km (5.5 miles) circular.
Start and Finish	Kilngreen car park by the Ewes Water, just north of the town centre. The walk is waymarked with a number 4 on wooden posts.
Terrain	Public road, forest track, grazed hillside path. Boots or strong shoes recommended.
Map	OS Explorer 323, Eskdale & Castle O'er Forest.
Refreshments	Reasonable choice in Langholm.
Opening Hours	Clan Armstrong Trust Museum: Easter-Oct, Tues, Wed, Fri-Sun: 14.00-17.00.

One day in the mid 1990s, management summoned the council rangers: 'Drop everything', they said, 'and go and look at Langholm.' We grinned among ourselves: what bright idea had they come up with now? And what was it about Langholm, anyway, that all current projects had to go on hold?

During the 18th century the 'Muckle Toon' was the largest, most prosperous centre in the Borders, benefiting from its gateway position and cross-border smuggling. The 20th-century poet, Hugh MacDiarmid, was born there. That was about the limit of my knowledge.

We went to Langholm and we looked. Then we did drop everything else and concentrated on the Muckle Toon. It was the dawn of the Langholm Walks Initiative. The project was not so much one of creating paths as of tweaking and promoting them—locals had been hiking the hills around their home town for centuries. Suddenly the penny had dropped: Langholm was a walker's paradise. This quiet, hitherto self-contained corner of the region could generate a disproportionate slice of tourist income.

For a while 'Langholm' and 'Walks Initiative' were flavour-of-the-month buzz words, sailing across polished table tops from one manager to another like Frisbees fresh out of cellophane. Finance was drawn down. On the ground, posts were put in holes and a system of numbered and waymarked walks appeared.

A decade, later it's hard to imagine Langholm without its path network. Countryside managers have moved on, gleefully high-fiving over dedicated mountain bike trails. Langholm, meanwhile, quietly benefits from its moment in the limelight. It now has its own walking festival and various walks booklets. As for the locals, they just do what they always did: take their favourite paths over the hills.

From the Kilngreen car park, walk upstream and cross the Ewes Bridge, soon passing between gate pillars and coming to the Clan Armstrong Centre. The Armstrongs were a famous Langholm family of Border reivers. Generations of them either lived in or were evicted from the castle, just across the racecourse. The turbulent times of cattle rustling and murder are catalogued there on an information panel, if you care for the detour.

The main outward trek follows a quiet estate driveway, starting wide and metalled between mature beeches and slowly lessening in grandeur until it becomes first a forest road and finally a hill track. Ignore turnings to left and right which lead to estate houses and farms. Just keep on the main track through woodland and alongside the Esk. You'll pass a large pheasant hatchery before the track begins to curve steadily round to the left, keeping with the river valley, finally breaking clear of mature trees. There are grand views over Eskdale to the hills beyond.

Just after the cottage of Potholm take a sharp right up a track, cross a stile by a gate and then follow the markers uphill with a fence on your right, aiming for the cleft between Wrae Hill and Potholm Hill. The ground levels out at Wrae Hass (a Norse name meaning 'fertile pass'). Some wind-stunted alder trees make a good landmark.

A series of stiles and the line of a fallen dyke guide you uphill. The views from Potholm are great. On one side the Ewes Water meanders along a bright green valley—you are looking out towards Teviotdale. To the other side, the valley of the larger River Esk finds its way between tight-packed hills. Apparently you can see 18 ancient earthworks from here—hill forts or entrenched settlements—but as you turn slowly about, attention is sidetracked by the general splendour of the surroundings. That's my excuse anyway. I could only see eight. Moreover, I'd just walked right through the middle of one as I came up the hill, without even noticing.

Langholm

Your course is straight along the hill top. Cross a ladder stile and soon begin dropping down onto Castle Hill, the dyke on your left now in stockproof condition. Where this wall goes sharp left keep straight on, descending amid hawthorn scrub. You now have an excellent view over Langholm. Especially seen from above it is a well-shaped town, its dimensions circumscribed by rolling hills rising all around, the layout dictated by three converging rivers. Mill chimneys still stand and the way the buildings nestle beneath the slopes is reminiscent of towns a little further east, across the county boundary in the Scottish Borders. From these surrounding hills—Whita with its tall monument, Mid Hill across the Esk, and Warb Law to the south—this view is the same and yet subtly changed. A complete circuit of the town, taking in five tops, can be done in a long day.

Descending through denser hawthorn scrub, head for the centre mass of the town, hit a track and bear slightly left downhill until the dyke can be crossed by a ladder stile. Pass Pathhead on the small road and continue back to the car park.

CAERLAVEROCK

Distance	5.5km (3.5 miles) circular.
Start and Finish	Free car park on the sea side of the B725, 800 metres west of Caerlaverock. From Dumfries, take the Glencaple Road south of the town, for about 13km/8 miles. Look out for a sign to Lantonside Farm on the left, the car park is 800 metres further on.
Terrain	All-abilities path, undefined path across salt-marsh, board-walks, farm tracks and public road. Boots or strong shoes recommended.
Map	OS Explorer 322, Annandale.
Refreshments	Caerlaverock Castle café, open same times as castle, rough-ly Apr-Sept, 9.30-18.30; Oct-Mar, 9.30-16.30. Adult entry fee to the castle is about £4.
Other Interest	Wildfowl and Wetlands Trust, Eastpark Farm, Caerlaverock. Especially if you want to see spectacular numbers of barna-cle geese, any time between Oct-Apr. WWT open all year, 10.00-17.00.

If you know someone who likes reading information boards, you must take them on this walk. Don't expect to get back for an early lunch. In fact, don't expect to get back for lunch at all. Tea time will be about right. By then your friend will have ingested so much information he'll be bloated and encyclopaedic on the natterjack toad.

From the car park an eerily smooth and wonderful path leads you along the side of the merse past various interpretation panels. This path stops suddenly and you're more or less on your own after that, though sometimes an old pallet or plank of wood has been po-sitioned over the deeper holes. This walk along the merse is great. Above the blowing grasses the town of Silloth is at eye level, 13km away across the Solway Firth, with Skiddaw and Grizedale looming above. It looks almost as if you could walk across to them.

In summer you can see the rare aforementioned toads here, small and light-coloured with a yellow back stripe. They hang out under bits of rubbish and make a racket if they're in the mood. The flowers and grasses are typical salt marsh; this whole area gets

Lanarkland

Dovecotwell

ROMAN
TEMPORARY
✝ CAMP

Ward
Law

⊙ Fort

MS

Shearin

antonside

Mains

26

B 725

Caerlaverock
Castle

L

Bowhouse

Start/Finish

6

P

Caerlaverock N

M

1km

Crown Copyright. 100031557

Caerlaverock Castle

covered by the highest spring tides. In the winter you might see barnacle geese, though they tend to feed further along the coast, near the Wildfowl and Wetland Trust Visitor Centre.

Just as the lack of information boards is beginning to erode your confidence, you come to a strange structure covered in tar-paper tiles. As bird hides go, this doesn't strike me as the most appealing. In fact, it's ugly. It must have some advantage, though. Perhaps it folds up when you pull a lever into something the size of a coffee table and can be wheeled away on a barrow.

You need to come off the merse here and walk up through the woods on a collection of boardwalks. You know you're on the right path now—the information panels get going again, giving you chapter and verse about the trees. The first thing of interest you come to is the site of the original castle. There's not much left of it, but a really good illustrated panel gives you all the detail you need about what originally stood here and why it was abandoned.

WALK 16

Now you have to make a choice. You can opt for a full inspection of Caerlaverock Castle itself. It's excellent and there is a lot to see, but quite expensive—the prices are displayed on a board. If you want to save your cash, you might choose to slink through, keeping to the track and heading beneath the sandstone arch for the road. This feels slightly deceitful but is perfectly legitimate. You can eye the castle wistfully out of the corner of your eye as you go.

Castles with significant curtain wall defences are not too common in this part of Scotland. There is one just north of Beattock (Auchen Castle). Threave, outside Castle Douglas, also had significant perimeter defences. Caerlaverock seems to look south of the border for its inspiration. Built by the Maxwell family in the 1270s, it confronts besieger and visitor alike with two gigantic gate towers, reminiscent of Dunstanburgh Castle in Northumberland. Having abandoned the eminently defensible site of the first castle (probably because the whole thing was sinking into the swamp) the builders of the second Caerlaverock probably reckoned to dent the psyche of their enemies by the sheer size of these prominences. Behind them, the triangular moated plan shape was described by a 14th-century soldier as, 'like a shield... surrounded by an arm of the sea'.

It was besieged on several occasions: by Robert the Bruce, Edward I and during the English Civil War. A new residential wing got totally trashed when the castle was taken in 1640.

When you've seen enough, head out to the road. For an added bonus, cross directly over and follow signs up to Ward Law, an Iron Age hill fort. The views from the top are tremendous. The Cumbrian shore and the hills behind are now plainly not such an easy walk away, the wide tidal Solway having become visible with the extra height. Red sandstone Caerlaverock sits solid among trees which become denser to the right, forming the ancient Castle Wood. You get an excellent view across to Criffel too, on the other side of the Nith estuary.

Return to the road and turn right. It's not a motorway and you're unlucky if you see as many as three cars in the 800 metres back to your parking place. Soon the road converges on the west

Flag Iris, Caerlaverock merse

end of Castle Wood. You can look into darkness among the trees
and speculate whether any of the gnarled oaks are old enough to
remember Caerlaverock inhabited.

WATERLOO MONUMENT

Distance	4km (2.5 miles) circular.
Start and Finish	Sweetheart Abbey car park, at the east end of New Abbey's main street.
Terrain	Public road, grazed field with waymarked path, steep stone steps, undefined and soft forest ride, farm track. Boots or strong shoes recommended.
Map	OS Explorer 313, Dumfries and Dalbeattie.
Refreshments	Tea room beside the abbey, pubs by the corn mill.
Opening Hours	Same as for corn mill and abbey: Apr-Sept, 09.30-18.30; Oct-Mar, 09.30-16.30.
Other Interests	Shambellie House Costume Museum: open Apr-Oct, 10.00-17.00.

Every village has history, if you care to search for it. New Abbey has so much, you don't have to search at all; you can park next to it, walk round it and buy it on postcards. That's the obvious, tourist-friendly sort of history—the abbey, the corn mill, Shambellie House costume museum and the picturesque houses along the main street, which huddle so closely together, they push out into the road and impede traffic flow.

New Abbey takes its name from the wonderful ruin of warm red sandstone, standing at the east end of the main street. 'New' is a relative term. Sweetheart Abbey was founded in 1273. It is, nevertheless, still the youngest of Galloway's three Cistercian Abbeys—Dundrennan goes back an extra hundred years. The 'sweet heart' of the abbey's name belonged to John Balliol, a 13th-century nobleman. He died in 1269 and his devoted wife, Lady Devorgilla de Balliol, had his heart cut out and embalmed. A special casket was delicately crafted for it out of silver and ivory. Then, wherever she went, his heart went too.

A remarkable and progressive woman, Devorgilla threw her energies into ambitious projects: the first bridge across the River Nith at Dumfries, Buittle Castle, Sweetheart Abbey, Balliol College in Oxford, Greyfriars and Blackfriars monasteries in Dumfries and

Sweetheart Abbey at sunset

Wigtown. She outlived her husband by 21 years. When she finally died at the then extraordinary age of 80, she and the heart were buried together in the abbey's church and the monks adopted the title Dulce Cor (Sweet Heart) for the home she had built them.

Sweetheart Abbey has a decent-sized car park and so is the best place to start and finish. Walk west along the main street, almost as far as the corn mill.

You need to get on the minor road which runs round the back of the mill pond, signposted 'Waterloo Monument'. At its end, follow a path up through the fields to a kissing gate which gives access to a steep flight of stone steps.

From the top the view of Nithsdale is spectacular. New Abbey nestles in the foreground and the cooling towers of Chapelcross nuclear power station, north of Annan, stand at the back. Climb the Waterloo Tower for an even more panoramic view. Refreshingly, Health and

Safety haven't managed to catch up with this monument yet. At the top you are not enclosed with view-restricting and unsightly barriers – instead it is left to your common sense to avoid plunging 20 metres onto a very hard-looking slab of bedrock.

This tower was built in 1816. The first motive was as stated on the plaque: 'To record the valour of those British, Belgian and Prussian soldiers who under Wellington and Blucher on the 18th June 1815 gained the victory of Waterloo by which French tyranny was overthrown and peace restored to the world.'

The more practical purpose in building it, and others of a similar kind, was to provide employment for local men returning from the wars. What with the hillside steps you've climbed and the very considerable labour resource needed to build the tower itself, I imagine it kept a good number of ex-soldiers out of trouble for quite a while.

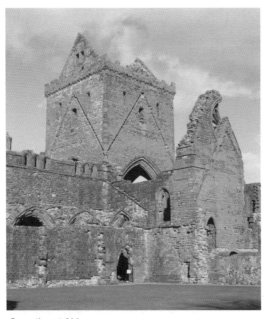

Sweetheart Abbey

Over the Solway from the top of Waterloo Tower

You can return to New Abbey the way you came, or you can take the path leading away northwards among trees. Descend steeply until you hit Carsegowan Farm track. Then, turning right, walk via the sawmill back to the village. A word of caution, though: as you near the bottom of the hill a superfluity of paths leading off in all directions can be confusing. As long as you keep going downhill you should end up on the track. These woods are due for harvesting soon. After that, who knows? The Forestry Commission may put in one of their quality waymarked trails.

CRIFFEL

Distance	Ardwall-Criffel top return, 4.5km (3 miles); Ardwell-Criffel top-Waterloo Monument car park, 6km (4 miles).
Start and Finish	Waterloo Monument car park, south of New Abbey, at the end of the minor road starting behind the corn mill. Or Ardwall car park—take the Southerness road (A710) south of New Abbey for about 3km/2 miles, then turn right, signposted for Craigbeg and Ardwell Mains. In 800 metres, the car park is on the right.
Terrain	Farm track, rough but well-defined hill path, steep slopes, forest track. Boots recommended.
Map	OS Explorer 313, Dumfries & Dalbeattie.
Refreshments	Pubs and tearoom in New Abbey. Nothing at Ardwall.

The name Criffel, or Crafel as it appears on 18th-century maps, is derived from old Scottish 'Craw's Fell'—Crow's Hill. Visitors to Dumfries cannot fail to notice the hill; it's the most obvious landmark this side of the Solway.

Looking at more recent maps, there might appear to be as many ways of walking on and off this hill as there are degrees of bearing on a compass. It's round-backed and there aren't too many steep drop-offs. By the time you've parked the car, however, the choice is more limited.

Route A starts at the Waterloo Monument car park south of New Abbey. Cross the bridge, skirt the gardens at Mid Glen, follow the forest track for a few metres and then turn left, heading straight up Knockendoch. The hard work is in getting up this pointed shoulder. From Knockendoch it's a stroll to the top of Criffel.

You *could* go up this way. Many others make the same mistake, so at least you won't flounder alone. Route A is a peaty gutter. If you want to give it a try, wait for a long drought. I've shown it on the map in blobs.

Route B is better. Also busy and with an established car park at Ardwall Mains, it tackles the east face of the hill, missing out Knockendoch. Head up the farm track between drystone dykes. The path

Start/Finish

1km

Crown Copyright. 100031557

Criffel from across the Nith

steepens, eroded by summit-hungry family outings. Alongside the Craigrockall Burn the soils have a higher mineral content, the granite bedrock breaking the surface. You have to scramble over numerous boulders. Some folk may start to have second thoughts before they've even cleared the unbeautiful areas of windblown and clearfell forestry. Once above the trees, just keep on up. If you thought the burn side was steep, it's nothing to the beeline you'll be making for the top.

You may be wondering why I've included Criffel in this book of 25 good walks. Has it anything to recommend it? Well, it's in because it's the most annoying hill *not* to have climbed. Every time you set eyes on it, you kick yourself for not having been up.

Criffel impresses, not because of its height above sea level, which at 569 metres isn't all that great, but because that height is seen in the Solway Firth's immediate context. Part of a Devonian volcanic system, it rises directly from a coastal fringe of green fields to tower above grey expanses of estuarine mud. From far out at sea a granite slab near the summit reflects sunlight—a legendary beacon for incoming ships.

From the top there's not much you can't see, the views are excellent. The big hills of the northern Lake District stand up, close and alluring. In the other direction a white lozenge catches your eye; it's Dumfries Infirmary, marking the southern edge of the town. Long

Fell curves round to the west, ending in the relatively minor volcanic blip of Lotus Hill with Loch Arthur at its foot. To the east, the straight seaward course of the River Nith is backed by the pretty undulating patchworks of Nithsdale and Annandale. The hardships of the climb have been worthwhile.

Descend the same way. Alternatively, you can leave a bike or second car at the Waterloo Monument car park, turning your expedition into a more interesting circuit. This allows you to descend via Knockendoch, giving the view variety.

Criffel top

Loch Kindar stretches below. One of its small forested islands has the remains of a chapel—Kirk Kindar. The other, nearer the middle, was a crannog. Many of the lochs in Dumfries and Galloway contained these man-made island dwellings. Reached by submerged causeways, they gave protection from wild beasts and unwanted callers. Now they're the ultimate in archaeological research. Owing to the low temperature of Scotland's lochs, wood, leather, seeds and bones survive for centuries, giving insights into the way crannog dwellers lived. Recently a 2,500-year-old wooden butter dish was discovered on a crannog site. There was still enough butter on it to spread a sandwich.

Descending Knockendoch on route A, the path becomes increasingly miry. The worst section lies below, on the forest ride, but you can avoid it. Turn left at a derelict dyke running off the shoulder to the west. This is a bit of a heathery scramble but at least it keeps you out of the gutter. Drop down to the forest road, turn right and, after roughly a kilometre, go left to Mid Glen and the Waterloo Monument car park.

The thing about Criffel is, once you've climbed it—experienced the hardships and admired the views—then, every time you look at it afterwards you get a sense of satisfaction. That round-backed whale of a hill, shining pink in the sunrise; you know what it's like up there. Life is enriched by the simplest things.

CARSETHORN TO POWILLIMOUNT

Distance	11km (7 miles) circular.
Start and Finish	Small car park at Carsethorn. Turn left off the A710 at Kirkbean, south of New Abbey. The village of Carsethorn lies at the end of this road. Turn right and the car park is on your left.
Terrain	Roads, farm tracks, shingle beach and rocks which can be quite slippery. Boots recommended.
Map	OS Explorer 313, Dumfries and Dalbeattie.
Refreshments	Carsethorn has a pub.
Opening Hours	John Paul Jones Museum: Apr-Sept, Tues-Sun, 10.00-17.00.

If you see people doing exaggerated cartwheels on the beach south of Carsethorn, you've probably spotted a party of palaeontologists. So exciting are the rock and fossil remains exposed here by the sea, anyone with so much as a whiff of science about them might be excused for emitting snatches of complete gibberish. But from the genuine academic, expect nothing short of gymnastics. This is, after all, Dinantian Stratigraphy in a nutshell—the Kirkbean Outlier of the Northumberland Trough.

From the village, get down onto the beach and head right, hopping over a couple of breakwaters. Ignore the fossils for a moment; this part of the beach is the best for birds. Large flocks of waders hang around on the water's edge and can be seen at close quarters. They will include dunlin and knot, but there may also be redshank, greenshank, plovers, curlew and avocet among the hundreds of oystercatchers and gulls. Their combined clamour adds dimension to the vast areas of tidal mud and the backdrop of the Lake District hills.

The walking is sometimes tricky, over rocks made slippery by algae and recent immersion. It's best done on a low or falling tide. At high water springs it won't be practicable at all; you'd probably have to give up on it.

Behind, views of the hills of Upper Nithsdale disappear as you make your way round Borron Point. Under your feet are layer upon layer of

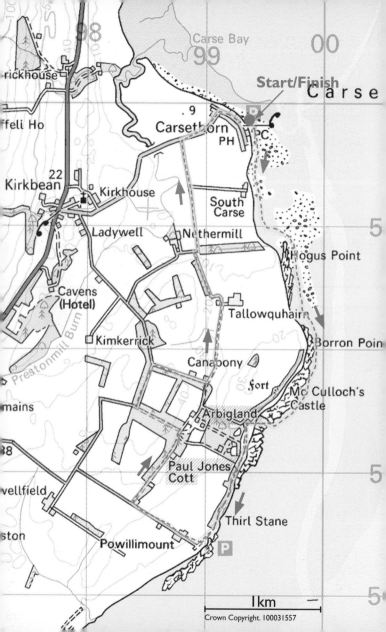

Carsethorn beach

Lower Carboniferous rocks, mudstones and sandstones, folded upwards by tectonic activity to expose a cross-section of geological time. As you progress along the shore, the rocks are generally getting older, displaying indicators of the conditions under which they were laid down—turbulent tidal shore, river delta, or warm shallow lagoon teeming with life. Even if, like me, you haven't a scoobie what you're looking at, you can't fail to be impressed. Your walk may get no further, especially if children are present, but degenerate into two hours stooped, searching for the ultimate fossil. Will it be a massive-headed Lithostrotion clavaticum or the gigantoproductid Caniniophyllum? Your guess is as good as mine.

Continue past the House on the Shore and the foot of Arbigland Gardens. Arbigland used to be one of the main landholding estates in this part of Galloway, but like others of its kind, it got hit by death duties.

Soon a path rises up onto the cliffs and winds among trees, then descends again to a massive lump of rock separated from the main cliffs and cleft through the middle with a natural arch. This is the Thirl Stane.

WALK 19

John Paul Jones' Cottage

As you approach a car park, you can look further south along the coast to Southerness, which has a holiday village and a very fine old lighthouse, one of the earliest built in Scotland, dating to 1748. Turn inland, following the road past Powillimount Farm. Then go right along a track past some cottages and Arbigland Estate's elaborate pets' graveyard. You come, eventually, to John Paul Jones' cottage.

Born here in 1747, John Paul was the son of a gardener at Arbigland House. From this inauspicious start (but with an intimate knowledge of the coast you have just walked), he became a great 18th-century seafarer and sailed all the oceans of the world.

At the age of 12, Jones took apprenticeship as ship's boy from the tiny port of Carsethorn. He rose to become commander of a merchant ship and amassed a fortune in the West Indies before offering his services to the embryonic American Navy. Britain became his employer's enemy and some of Jones' most famous sea battles were fought around his home coasts.

During a three-hour engagement off Flamborough Head in 1779, over half the crews of the opposing fleets were killed or injured. Jones, asked if he wished to surrender, replied: 'Surrender?

I have not yet started to fight.' In victory, but sinking, he transferred his men to a British warship and sailed for Holland with 500 prisoners.

His exploits read rather like those of Thomas Cochrane, though his ability as a naval commander and later as admiral were better appreciated, and his career was not blighted as Cochrane's was, by the obstructive prejudices of the British naval hierarchy. In France, Holland and Russia, Jones was a hero. In Britain, his actions against the establishment branded him a pirate. Fearless conqueror or ruthless villain—it all depended whose side you were on. Not even John Paul Jones managed to please everyone.

At his birthplace, a quarter of a millennium on, the Scottish and American flags fly side by side. It's a peaceful place. The stench of treachery which once hung over Jones' affiliations no longer seems to be a problem. Turn left near the gates of Arbigland House, right at the corner of the public road and left again down the farm track to Canabony and Tallowquhairn. This brings you onto the road just east of Nethermill, from where it is a straightforward stroll back into the village.

ROUGH FIRTH

Distance	Kippford to Rockcliffe and back via the Muckle Lands, 4km (2.5 miles) circular. Kippford to Rockcliffe via Muckle Hill, returning via Rough Island, 6.5km (4 miles) circular.
Start and Finish	Car park opposite Kippford Sailing Club's dinghy park (with toilets). Kippford is 6km/3.5 miles south of Dalbeattie, turning right off the A710.
Terrain	Public road, surfaced path, steep but defined hill path, estuarine mud. Boots or wellingtons recommended.
Map	OS Explorer 313, Dumfries & Dalbeattie.
Refreshments	Tearoom in Rockcliffe.

One of the great things about the Solway Firth is that you can walk on the mud. Where this is possible, getting offshore gives the most amazing feeling of freedom and space. If you are not accustomed to mud walking, Rough Firth is a good place to start as the surface is mostly quite firm, there are no deep channels to cross and there's the bonus of a causeway between Rough Island and the beach near Kippford.

Park at Kippford, next to the toilets opposite the sailing club. Then walk along to the bus shelter past the two pubs, the chandlers and the lifeboat station. Turn left by the small shop/ex-post office, uphill from the south end of the village and follow the road round until it becomes the Jubilee Path, created to celebrate Queen Victoria's umpteenth year on the throne.

If you want an easy walk, you can stroll to Rockcliffe and back along the Jubilee Path. It benefits from a considerable maintenance budget, courtesy of the National Trust for Scotland. However, if you want more of a scramble you need to turn off the Jubilee Path to the left, soon after leaving the village. Look for a path crossroads and a large boulder, just before you go under some power lines. This left turn leads you beneath a beautifully spreading oak tree and up a short steep climb to the top of the Muckle Hill.

Muckle means 'big' or 'much' in old Scots but it's nothing of a hill, so perhaps the adjective refers to the view. From the top you can see Bengairn and Screel Hill to the north-west, and the rich Urr Valley stretching inland

Rough Island

from Palnackie. To the south the view takes in the breadth of the Muckle Lands and beyond them the bay of Rough Firth spreads out with Rough Island in the middle, and the Lake District hills behind. In view terms it's about as good as it gets for a climb of only 100 metres.

Carry on along the length of the hill top and descend among gorse bushes. It's less steep than the ascent. When you come back to the Jubilee Path, turn left towards Rockcliffe and after a while go right, following a sign for Mote of Mark. From the top of this little fort plateau you can get a similar but slightly less spectacular view over the firth. In the Mote Meadows there's an interpretation board describing Mark's Mote and informing nervous householders about vitrification. That's where the woodwork of a building burns so fiercely it melts the stones together: every loss-adjuster's nightmare. It appears to have happened to King Mark.

Crossing the Mote Meadows diagonally away from the road, you reach Rockcliffe village with its popular beach. There are public toilets and benches to sit on if the weather is fine.

If the tide is out or on the ebb, you have a choice. Both return options are shown on the map, but my preference is to walk out across the mud, heading for the landward tip of Rough Island. NTS ask you not to go across during the nesting season, especially with dogs, which eat the eggs and young of ground-nesting birds. Ringed plovers lay their eggs on the island's shingle beaches and common terns nest on the short cropped grass.

Trying to improve the nesting habitat for the ringed plovers once got me into bother. The idea is to clear vegetation from large areas of shingle so that the birds can build their nests away from predator-concealing cover. It's a mattock and spade job, absolutely

Mote of Mark

backbreaking, particularly if you're a volunteer and being driven on by a ranger with some sort of crazy work-till-you-die ethic.

When the tide started to come in, the labour continued without respite. Our reward would be that the decline in numbers of nesting pairs might be reversed that season. The downside was, the rangers would be in traction.

When the tide lapped at the causeway, the ranger still refused to call it a day. His volunteer, beginning to look decidedly jumpy, suggested they make a run for it, rather than stop the night on the island. 'Just finish this small area,' the ranger said. 'Then we'll down tools. See, it'll only take a moment!'

It's surprising how quickly the causeway covers with a west wind driving the tide up the Solway. By the time we set out, where to walk was a matter of guess work. The sea water in March is cold, especially when the waves slap around your waist. Sometimes apologies just aren't enough. After that early blunder, I've always treated my volunteers with great consideration.

Arriving at the beach, the walk is completed by returning to your car along the single-track road. You'll pass a collection of sea-inspired sculpture en route. Some like it, some don't. Children mostly do.

WALK 20

HESTAN ISLAND

Distance	7.5km (4.5 miles).
Start and Finish	Drive to Auchencairn along the A711, turning left at the bottom of the village, signposted Balcary Bay. 2km/1.5 miles down there is a parking space on the right. Start by walking south along the road for a hundred metres or so, until you can get down easily onto the mud.
Terrain	Mud, grazed turf, undefined path. Boots or wellingtons recommended. THIS WALK SHOULD ONLY BE UNDERTAKEN AT VERY LOW TIDE AND IN SETTLED, FINE WEATHER.
Map	OS Explorer 313, Dumfries & Dalbeattie.
Refreshments	Balcary Bay Hotel or Auchencairn.

Not too many people fancy walking to Hestan. And yet, of all the islands off the coast of Galloway, it is perhaps the most alluring. It tempts you from so many places—a green hummock surrounded by blue sea; a distant, secret place, basking in the sun.

Without a boat, landfall on Hestan means either a long walk down to Almorness Point and a sticky crossing to the Rack, or negotiating the tidal mud across Auchencairn Bay. The Council Ranger Service used to offer guided walks to Hestan by the latter route, advertising them 'Not for the faint-hearted'. This proviso, it was hoped, would discourage large numbers. Unfortunately the fearless rose to the challenge, arriving in strength. Eventually the walk was discontinued, a victim of its own success. Nevertheless, with certain precautions, people can reach Hestan Island by themselves.

First, get the tides right. Choose the biggest daytime spring from a current Solway Tide Table—a 9.9 metres is adequate. This gives very low water levels at low tide and plenty of time to walk out, look round the island and return. Allow three hours, to be safe.

Second, keep a close eye on the weather. If it's bad, forget it.

Among the stuff you normally take on walks, make sure you have a compass, a mobile phone and three pieces of 12 inches x 10 inches board, about half an inch (12mm) thick—sterling board is ideal. The compass will keep you on course. Coastal fog is unnerving if it catches you out on mud flats. As for the mobile phone; if disaster occurs, call the coastguard.

The boards help to avoid making that embarrassing call. Most of the surface between Hestan and the mainland is hard, but you shouldn't take estuarine mud for granted. The boards are light and easy to carry. If you find yourself getting bogged, use them to spread your weight while you beat a retreat. Wear wellingtons, if you've a comfortable pair. When you get to the burn, they'll mean you can cross straight over.

All this sounds rather off-putting but don't be dissuaded, either by the precautions or by the mud at the start. Just offshore it's sticky, but 50 metres out it firms up nicely. Mud-walking is half the pleasure of this expedition; a vast emptiness of ripple-marked plopping ooze, surrounded by distant hills.

Make a beeline, not for Hestan Island itself but midway between north Hestan and Almorness Point. Reach the Chapel Croft Lane, a small burn cutting the mud to the west of Hestan Rack. The sides of the burn can be soft. Don't stand around admiring the view and arguing how to spell guillemot, keep your feet moving. After casting around for a good place, cross the burn. It won't be deep except after heavy rain. Test the depth, anyway, with a stick.

Once on the causeway you are home and dry. The Rack is a naturally occurring sweep of stones, topped by a bed of blue mussels. Mark your crossing place.

Hestan—called Rathen's Island in S.R. Crockett's novel *The Raiders*—has lots to see. The cottage was last permanently inhabited during the 1960s by a church organ-maker and his wife, whose duties in taking the island's tenancy included keeping the lighthouse lit and looking after the affairs of miscreant sheep. They spent three years here, plagued by rats. The organ-maker's wife wrote a book about their experiences.

In the 14th century, Hestan was called Estholm, meaning East Grazing. A narrow rectangular enclosure remains from that time, situated on the north-facing slope. Records of 1348 have this as the Pele Tower of Duncan McDowell, a prominent Galloway chief-

Hestan Elephant

tain and Balliol sympathiser. The stronghold was probably built to provide a bolthole for various Balliols, their castle at Buittle having been trashed by Robert the Bruce in 1313. If you had aspirations to the Scottish throne, the natural defences of a place like Hestan came in handy.

The first lighthouse was built in 1893 following a spate of shipwrecks. The current version, dating from 1996, is solar-powered. From the lighthouse, follow the cliffs to the right. Below you cormorants stand on rocks, stretching their wings. The close-cropped, guano-enriched grasslands are the result of centuries of gulls dropping and sheep grazing.

An unexpected herbivore inhabits the beach towards the north end of the west shore. This is the Hestan Elephant, a free-standing sea pillar, weather-eroded to bulk-and-trunk likeness. Nearby are the man-made caves of an unsuccessful copper mine.

Hestan Island

Back on the Rack and over the Lane, your judgement will have been perfect if the tide on your left has hardly turned. As you re-trace your steps across the mud, Hestan recedes. It loses none of its mystic qualities for closer inspection. As the gulls settle down again behind, the island's allure returns to the backward glance.

PALNACKIE AND ORCHARDTON

Distance	9km (5.5 miles) circular.
Start and Finish	Palnackie is just off the A711, about 5km/3.5 miles out of Dalbeattie. Once in the village, drive down Port Road, opposite the Glen Isle Inn. There is a car park near the water's edge.
Terrain	Road, farm track, merse, old drove road, forest path. Boots or strong shoes recommended.
Map	OS Explorer 313, Dumfries & Dalbeattie.
Refreshments	The Glen Isle Inn, Palnackie. There is also the Crow's Nest, a restaurant next to the village stores, but its status at the time of writing is uncertain.
Other Interests	The North Glen glass-blower is definitely worth a visit.

The village of Palnackie has a small, mud-locked quay. Sailing ships used to arrive here, either to unload or to be warped on the making tide upriver to the main port of Dalbeattie. Consumables came in, Dalbeattie granite went out. The granite was of such high quality it ended up all over the world. The railways put a stop to it in the second half of the 19th century. The two ports struggled on for a while before being abandoned.

Walk through the village centre and turn left, up a small road climbing among fields with views over the River Urr towards Kippford. If you've extra time on your hands you can stop at North Glen's glass-blowing workshop where you can buy individually crafted glassware, too, if you can see your way to carrying it unscathed round Almorness.

The road becomes a track, descending past South Glen. The big field after the farm used to be cut for silage. Being so close to sea level the state of the tide was critical. Cut grass at high water, and the weight of the tractor caused the surface of the field to roll in a series of waves. It was better to cut at low tide, not to risk breaking the surface tension. The round concrete things are drainage inspection chambers not, as some believe, air ducts to a ministerial bunker.

Beyond the field's seaward boundary, veer right to cross the merse, joining a track running round the bay (if walking this circuit in reverse, be sure to turn out onto the merse). This must once have been a busy

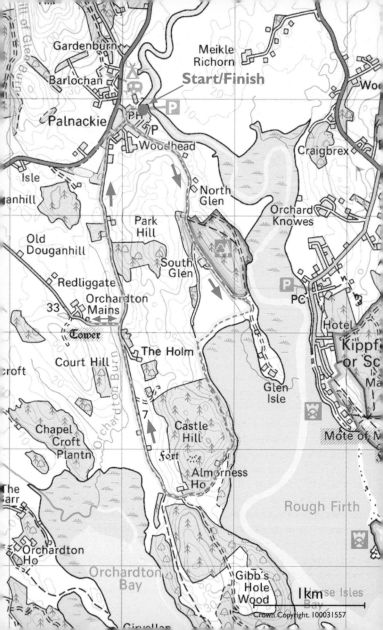

North Glen Glass-blower

thoroughfare for cart and animal traffic. Now it is wet underfoot and overgrown, eventually losing itself completely in the undergrowth at the foot of the sea cliff. The path takes a new line, rising above the track.

Oaks have been coppiced in these woods. The resultant rapid production of straight-grained timber could be used for fuel or charcoal-burning, building and furniture making. The place would have been a hive of activity. Now the woods are quiet. In early summer the bluebells are great.

This path has been kept open by local people who were rather taken with the idea that it might be put in *25 Walks*. Over the past 40 years it has fallen into decline so the way they saw it, perhaps some publicity might revive its fortunes. Especially in summer, it is inclined to become overgrown with bracken, hazel shoots and worst of all, brambles. The more people walk a path, the less chance the brambles have of taking it over. A stout stick might come in handy.

Further along the headland, the path joins a benched cart track again, which contours the slope and eventually brings you out at a cottage called Cocklehaen. Beyond that a more established vehicle track leads you onto a private road, running between mature oaks past Almorness House, part of the Keswick Estate.

As you turn north you get views towards Screel and Ben-gairn. Between the road and Orchardton Bay is a small private airfield. There is a white pole from which a windsock can be hung and the grass is kept in a state of aeroplane-friendly smoothness by close-cropping sheep. If the windsock is up it may be worth waiting to see if a plane comes in.

A kilometre up the road, Orchardton Tower is just off to the left. This unique building is in the care of Historic Scotland. Built for the Cairn family,

Orchardton Tower

lairds of Orchardton Estate in the 1450s, it's the only round tower house in the whole of Scotland.

Why the Cairns decided to build round instead of square or L-shaped is unknown. There's always someone who'll try something different. In this case I can't help thinking our gain in beholding its uniqueness was the laird's loss. Compared to the dwelling space offered by most rectangular towers, the circular rooms inside Orchardton are hardly of cat-swinging proportions, which might have been viewed as a serious oversight in the entertainment-loving 15th century. Especially when added to the nagging annoyance of her ladyship having no obvious place to put her linen chest.

As was common in fortified buildings of the time, the wall design of Orchardton Tower has been exploited for extra space. Garderobes, closets and even the main staircase were contained within their thickness. Climbing the narrow turnpike stairs dispels any preconceived ideas you might have about the eating and drinking habits of wealthy noblemen. Only a slimline laird could have negotiated the turns.

The ruinous buildings adjoining the tower were added to address spatial deficiencies. They comprised a great hall, brewhouse,

Rough Firth

bakery, stabling and storage. No architectural adventures this time, just straightforward rectangles.

After admiring Orchardton, retrace your steps as far as the T-junction, turning left along the quiet road back to Palnackie.

WALK 22

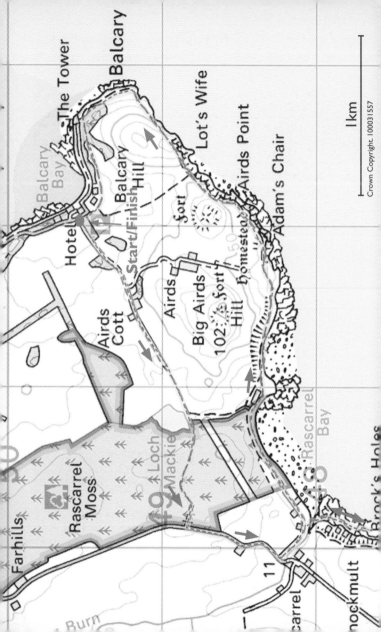

Crown Copyright. 100031557

1km

BALCARY TO RASCARREL

Distance	8km (5 miles) circular.
Start and Finish	Turn left off the A711 at the bottom of Auchencairn village, and drive down to the end of the road at Balcary Bay. Free parking is available behind the hotel.
Terrain	Farm track across grazed meadows, woodland path, forest road, shingle beach and cliff-top path (beware any children in your party or, for that matter, anyone suffering from vertigo!). Boots or strong shoes recommended.
Map	OS Explorer 313, Dumfries & Dalbeattie.
Refreshments	Balcary Bay Hotel.

Any path which forms a natural circuit is a joy to me. Balcary to Rascarrel is a good example. Not only is it a spectacular coastal path, it is actually three circuits in one, so you can choose a walk to suit the time available and how you feel on the day. The main circuit is described here, but the alternative shortcuts within it are fairly obvious on the ground and are shown on the map.

From the car park, walk up the farm track, signposted 'Right of Way to Loch Mackie and Rascarrel Bay', passing a small rookery on your right and Airds Cottage with its redundant kennels on your left. Mackie is a fisherman's loch, created by damming a burn. Now that the conifers behind have been felled, it provides the foreground for good views of Screel and Bengairn. Pass the loch and enter the woods, eventually turning left at a forest track, then left again once you come to the public road. This takes you down towards the sea between rolling green fields.

Just before Rascarrel Farm take another left along a small track leading to the shore. There's a parking space and a stout wooden footbridge crossing the Rascarrel Burn. If you wish you can go over this bridge heading south. There are some interesting rock features at Brock's Holes, just beyond the first bay—among them the slenderest of natural arches. Return to the main circuit of the walk, passing a cave beneath the cliff and rejoining the vehicle track servicing holiday cottages around Rascarrel Bay.

Caves along this shore are known to have been used by smugglers in the 17th and 18th centuries. Balcary Bay was notoriously busy, every variety of taxable import being brought in under cover of darkness. From most people's perspective, there was no harm in it. The Reverend John Steven, minister of Mochrum in the 1790s, light-heartedly attributed the burgeoning birth rate among his parishioners and even the improved state of agriculture to smuggling. Massive quantities of tea, spirits, tobacco, silk and salt were shipped to the Isle of Man, where customs duties were minimal. Most of it was destined for contraband receivers on the Solway coast. Brought ashore in small fast wherries, the goods were hidden in caves and purpose-built hides until they could be sold inland, the supply chain oiled by non-payment of customs. Law-abiding traders couldn't compete, so they turned tax-free too. The government were the only losers, but try finding someone who cared!

Not all smuggling stories ended happily, though. During the 1780s a Manx man was trying to earn extra money for his forthcoming wedding. After encountering contrary winds, he came into the Solway later than planned and was spotted by an excise cutter from Balcary Bay, running his illicit cargo of French brandy into Rough Firth. What to do? Giving himself up meant postponing the wedding indefinitely and bringing down on himself the concerted wrath of the authorities, his fiancée and his prospective mother-in-law. The intrepid smuggler made a run for the shore, whereupon the cutter's crew overhauled his wherry and shot him dead. His betrothed and both bickering families turned up soon after to claim the body, but while they were sailing it home for burial, their boat was hit by a freak squall off Hestan. With too many captains aboard and not many sailors, the steering was mismanaged. The vessel capsized and all were drowned.

Along the shore track at Rascarrel you head towards Airds Point. Old barytes workings are evident, with spoil heaps near the beach. This greenish or pinkish mineral was mined mainly for the manufacture of white paint.

The best of the walk is still to come. Climbing to the cliff top the path now begins a spectacular roller-coaster above the sea, the sheer, lichen-covered rock faces exposed to view ahead in increasingly dramatic form. Various features stand out, such as the huge

opposite page: View from the cliff path

Airds Point

slab of Adam's Chair. Further along there is the white, guano-encrusted sea pillar of Lot's Wife and further round again, Hestan Island comes into view from Balcary Point. The rugged rocks at the island's southern tip are called Daft Anne's Steps. The story goes that Anne was a schoolgirl of suppressed intelligence whose obsession was to cross Balcary Bay on stepping stones. Needless to say, after several failed attempts and lacking the luxury of modern tide tables, she drowned.

In the spring, nesting seabirds can be seen—especially fulmars, which choose nest sites high on cliff walls. They glide out along the edges on straight wings.

The path rounds Balcary Point and brings you back past the old Lifeboat House, now a private dwelling. On leaving the woods, keep out from the right hand edge of the field, otherwise you won't find the kissing gate in the bottom corner, which brings you back to the Balcary Bay car park.

SCREEL HILL AND BENGAIRN

Distance	8.5km (5.5 miles) linear or 11km (7 miles) circular if you haven't managed to arrange transport for the return stretch along A711.
Start and Finish	Screel Hill car park, just off the A711. After passing Palnackie on the left, go a further 4km/2.5 miles before turning right up a minor road. The car park is signposted by the Forestry Commission, on the left.
Terrain	Forest road, well-defined and waymarked hill path, soft and undefined forest ride, undefined hill path over heather, old drove road, public road. Boots recommended.
Map	OS Explorer 312, Kirkcudbright and Castle Douglas. This has good coverage of 99% of the walk, though annoyingly misses out the car park (which lies on sheet 311).
Refreshments	Pubs in Auchencairn and Palnackie.

Screel Hill is an easy climb. It's waymarked by the Forestry Commission and so well walked you're unlikely to go wrong—just follow the signs of stampede to the top, up a mixture of forest road and steep stony path. Since a severe storm in 1998 a lot of trees have come out, so a route which used to be dark and enclosed is now much improved, the views increasingly spectacular as you ascend.

There's only one moment of doubt. Shortly before you break out above the trees, a particularly black stand of conifers is reminiscent of Screel in the 1990s. The path ascends into it, sunshine one moment, night the next. You can't see or hear anything. You know you've got to go up, but the way immediately ahead appears to be an impenetrable latticework of trunks and dead side branches. The route is actually off to the left, and there is a waymarker in among the trees. If you don't find it fairly quickly, better turn back and try again. According to the 1:25,000 OS map, a forest track runs all the way to the summit of Screel. This isn't really the case.

The top of Screel is split in two, the higher point being at the cairn to the west. The best views, however, are from the east end. Along the Solway, the Lake District hills stand up. Criffel dominates the north shore with the tiny stick of Southerness lighthouse

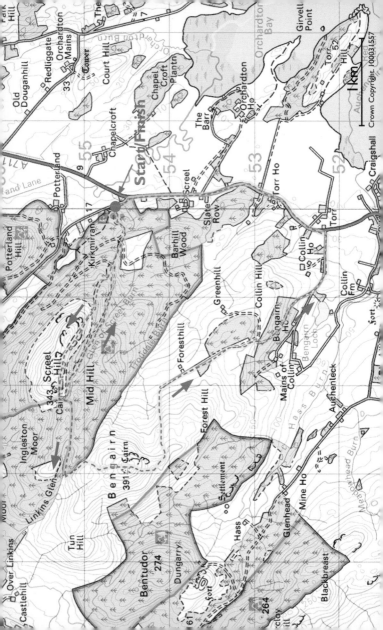

Bog Cotton on Screel, Bengairn beyond

at its foot. Rough and Hestan Islands bask in the near shallows of the firth.

Between Screel's twin tops a grassy path runs through soft hollows of waving bog cotton. From the cairn you get a good view to the north. If Screel was all you wanted, return the way you came up. Or, if you like to descend a different way, follow a steep downward path from the cairn. This enters the woods next to a dyke, then turns left along a waymarked trail through the trees, eventually coming to a forest road alongside the Glen of Screel Burn. Turn right when you meet the path you came up on.

For a more adventurous walk, ignore the left-pointing waymarker by the dyke and continue behind Mid Hill, heading for Bengairn. Having become used to an established path, this doesn't look too promising. In fact, it looks like it might be uncomfortable going. Follow the dyke, rising a little, then descending the Linkins Glen. Your suspicions are confirmed. You have to cast around continually to avoid swamps and windblown trees. The seepage of rank water through ageing boots reassures—there are pockets of wilderness left, and you're standing in the middle of one. You won't get lost, as long as you keep returning to the dyke.

Wild violets grow here, and insectivorous butterwort. The latter broadcasts its position with a bright yellow-green floret of leaves. From its centre, about the middle of June, a single flower stalk emerges, topped by a purple head, outlandishly appealing. Small bugs stick to its leaves and are chemically consumed. Their mineral content makes up for the impoverished bog soils

Linkins Glen

upon which the plant survives. If you are floundering in a peaty, insect-infested hole and come across butterwort, take heart—the black specks on its leaves are probably midges experiencing purgatory.

After about 800 metres, and just as you are coming to open ground, the dyke has collapsed. Cross to the other side of it and approach a junction of walls by the burn. There's no stile here but, being extra careful not to displace any stones, you can straddle a derelict hurdle to gain the open hill. Turn left, following the dyke up the side of the plantation. A couple of hundred metres' steep climb brings you to the corner of the wood and alongside another dyke, backed by an electric fence. Keeping this on your left, head uphill. The dyke is down in several places. At one point, a short distance along, some stones have been positioned to make an easy crossing of the fence.

Great care is needed here. It's not a big fence; in fact, you'll hardly touch it as you step over. But you don't want to have a leg either side of a hill fence before you discover it's got the mains running through it. To avoid getting, in a manner of speaking, an extra bolt through your undercarriage, test it first with a blade of grass. If there's a current, and you feel a reduced pulse through the stem, temporarily insulate the fence with a jacket or sweater. While making sure it doesn't do you any damage, make equally sure you don't damage it—the fence is restricting stock from ranging free.

Once across, the summit of Bengairn is an easy climb. The trig pillar stands 50 metres higher than the cairn on Screel. A low wall surrounds it, rather like that at the top of the Merrick.

No set path exists for your descent. The general idea is to make for Foresthill, the ruinous holding on the plain below. The best way of getting there, minimising the distance you have to walk through bracken and taking the more gradual slope, is to go south along the Bengairn ridge a few hundred metres, then come off the ridge to the east, heading well to the left of Foresthill. There is a gate into the northern-most enclosure, on the turfed-over line of an old drove road which runs off the hill. This takes you past the derelict farm and down.

Foresthill

Eventually the track bends abruptly to the right. Follow it round before passing left through some big double gates. Then continue down between mature woodlands. The track gains a metalled surface and drops towards the coast.

At the main road just outside Auchencairn, turn left and walk along the A711 back to your car. This is quite a slog, though mediated by wide mown verges. The trick is to avoid it altogether. If there are enough of you, a second car can have been left on the edge of Auchencairn, or simply drop off a bike in the hedge. Cycling along the road past Screel Farm only takes a couple of minutes and uses a different set of muscles to the ones you've been pounding the last few hours.

The view from Bengairn is not so very different from that on Screel. In fact, in some ways it's probably inferior. So why bother with Bengairn and all its hardships?

The great thing about having climbed both hills is the contrast. Screel's path is well-worn and waymarked. Everyone's been up Screel. Bengairn, on the other hand—the bigger of the two—is an untrampled wilderness of heather, blaeberry and grass. From the windswept top, look back towards Screel and remember the deep, steady silence of the forest behind Mid Hill; flies dancing in sunshine above a soggy ride, the close blackness between conifer trunks. You have seen what is hidden and surmounted what is seen. Afterwards you might ache a bit, but adding Bengairn to Screel turns a good walk into a great one.

GLENSONE AND THE MAIDEN

Distance	10km (6 miles) circular.
Start and Finish	Leave Dalbeattie by the B793, signposted for Caulkerbush. In about 10km/6 miles a turning downhill on the left is sign-posted for several farms, among them Glensone, Ryes and Bogknowe. Take this road and find a place to park on the verge, either near the junction or near Bogknowe Bridge
Terrain	Farm road, farm track, waymarked but not well-defined path over grazed farmland, undefined path over heather moor-land, forest road, public road. Boots or strong shoes recommended.
Map	OS Explorer 313, Dumfries & Dalbeattie.
Refreshments	Nothing near so take food and drink with you.
Opening Hours	The Gliding Club is open all year, Sunday afternoons.

This is a walk for a warm Sunday afternoon. Park on wide verges near the Bogknowe Bridge, just off the B793. The bridge crosses the South-wick Burn. A little further downstream this watercourse is good for amethysts. You can search among the rocks and find quite large lumps of purple semi-precious stone, not as pure as you can buy in your local gem shop, but a lot nicer for having discovered it yourself.

At Bogknowe Bridge, turn up a long straight lane running between dykes. Pass Glensone Farm and bear right towards Parkhead before turning left up a short track to a gate. At this junction there is a green painted arrow on a large boulder. The path was put in by the farmer at Glensone to encourage walkers in the wake of the Foot and Mouth outbreak of 2001. You can follow his markers almost to the top of Maidenpap. If the day has turned showery, take shelter in a small, purpose-built hut at the point where the path passes through the dyke. After that the climb onto the Maiden is straightforward. Just keep going up.

Heather does not make for easy walking. Mature calluna clumps, standing nearly a metre high, impede progress as if designed for the purpose, requiring massive energy input. But as we're constantly being advised to take more exercise, a bit of hard graft can't be bad. Beat obesity: come heather-hopping!

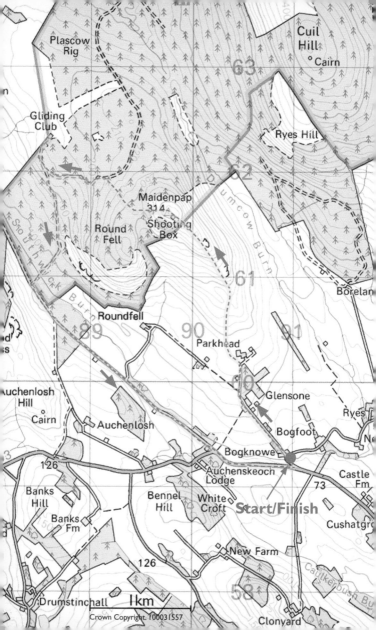

You'd think you had the hill all to yourself, but it's surprising what you can come across, hidden among heather. A deer-shooter once lay down for a nap on the Maiden. He awoke to see a walker hurrying downhill. As he approached, this walker kept looking at his watch, as if he could not believe the lateness of the hour, or perhaps his Rolex was broken. Glancing at his own watch, the deer-shooter called out helpfully, 'It's just gone 10.30.'

The walker stopped dead. A voice confirming his doom appeared to have come from the sky. Never spying the hidden shooter, he set off again downhill at an even faster pace, stumbling as he ran, a look of indescribable horror on his face. From which behaviour the shooter deduced, this man must be late for his own wedding. He should have been walking up the aisle at 10.30, not messing around on an old Maiden. Hell to pay, when he showed up.

From the top the views are excellent. Though it's only small, the Maiden is a fine hill, like a miniature Bengairn. Take a moment to inspect the shooting box by the trig pillar. This wasn't a grouse butt, from which shooters blasted off at driven birds, but a hilltop tearoom for post-shoot refreshment.

All the servants at the big house were given a day off to climb the Maiden. Their task was to carry massive quantities of food, beer and wine up to the shooting box for the enjoyment, as they laughingly put it, of the la-di-dahs. A table was suspended from the roof on chains. It was loaded with food and hauled up on pulleys into the ceiling. When the shooters had sufficiently reduced the grouse population they repaired to the shooting box, lowered the table and hey presto, there was the meal, ready laid out. Now open to the sky, the shooting box is a wind-scoured relic of a bygone age.

Descend steeply off the hill among heather to find a break in the trees leading to a dyke. Turn right, following it down to the forest road where a left turn leads you to a junction signposted, 'Dumfries and District Gliding Club'. A few hundred metres up you'll come to a hangar and a clubhouse, all delightfully low-budget. If you're interested, and if it's Sunday, the weather's good, an instructor is present and luck is on your side, you'll be offered a trial flight at an exceptionally low price.

The shooting box

This club dates from the days when gliding was in its infancy and take-off from a big hill was the only way to get a decent flight. The glider you'll probably fly is a K2, a German design dating from the 1950s. After the Second World War, Germany wasn't allowed to develop anything resembling military aircraft, so put its considerable expertise into producing gliders. K2s make ideal club trainers, having dual controls and being easily maintained.

Another airfield in Scotland runs a gliding school flying similar classics. Until recently this school was led by a Chief Flying Instructor of fierce reputation. He drove his pupils unremittingly until they were ready to fly solo, at which point he would take off with them, then unscrew the joystick from the rear pilot position, show it to the pupil sitting in the front seat and throw it out of the window, leaving the pupil in sole charge of the aircraft. 'You have control', he would say. The exciting thing about a glider is, you only get one go at landing it.

A pupil learning with this instructor got wind of his idiosyncrasy. 'Don't panic,' he was advised, 'if you're suddenly left on your own to land the plane.' The very next flight, the instructor tapped his pupil on the shoulder, showed him the blue-painted wooden joystick which he had stealthily unscrewed from its operational position, and popped it out of the sliding Perspex window.

The pupil grinned back happily. Then, following his instructor's example, he unscrewed his stick and threw it out of the window as well. The glider flew on peacefully without anyone in control of it at all, except the instructor, who after several minutes' silent reflection, began to work the rudder pedals as if he were riding a bicycle. When the glider was nearing the ground the pupil withdrew a third joystick from a hiding place inside his jacket, screwed it into position and made a perfect landing. The CFI has since retired.

From the top of the winch launch the view is amazing, and flying with only the sound of the wind is an experience you can get hooked on. 'We'll head for the Maiden,' the instructor might say and, as you soar above the tiny rectangle of the shooting box, 'Place your hand on the stick—now, you have control.'

When you've come back to earth you can resume your Sunday afternoon walk, descending the forest track to the minor road. Turn left, making your way between forests of young birch and pungent beds of bog myrtle. Skirting the bottom of Round Fell, you get a good view across to the hill you've just climbed. Pass the ruined cottages of Walltrees and Burnbank, turning left at the road junction where a Coronation horse trough dribbles slime into a bowl, and left again to reach your car at Bogknowe Bridge.

K2 being towed back to the hanger

The Solway Firth from the Maiden

INDEX

123

Also available in this series:

25 Walks: Arrochar, Cowal and Bute

25 Walks: Ayrshire and Arran

25 Walks: Chilterns

25 Walks: Cotswolds

25 Walks: Deeside

25 Walks: Edinburgh and Lothian

25 Walks: Fife

25 Walks: Heart of Scotland

25 Walks: Highland Perthshire

25 Walks: In and Around Aberdeen

25 Walks: In and Around Belfast

25 Walks: In and Around Glasgow

25 Walks: In and Around London

25 Walks: In Down District

25 Walks: Loch Lomond & Trossachs

25 Walks: Scottish Borders

25 Walks: Skye and Kintail

25 Walks: Yorkshire Dales